THE THOUSAND SONGS OF LORD VISHNU

by

Jeannette Caruth

SAI TOWERS

PUBLISHING

First Edition, 1998

ISBN-81-86822-42-9

Published & Distributed by :
Sai Towers Publishing
(A Unit of Sri Sathya Sai Towers Hotels Pvt Ltd.)
3/497 Main Road
Prasanthi Nilayam - 515 134
INDIA
Tel : 91-8555-87880
Fax : 91-8555-87302
EMail : saitower@giasbg01.vsnl.net.in

Contact for Mail Order in U.S.A.
JAI SAI RAM
PO Box 900
Trinidad, CO 81082 U.S.A.
Phone : (719) 846-0846
Fax : (719) 846-0847
E-Mail : jaisairm @ ria.net
OR
jaisairm @ rmi.net

Printed by :
D.K. Fine Arts Press Pvt. Ltd.
New Delhi - 110 052

I LAY THESE THOUSAND SONGS OF LOVE

AT THE

GOLDEN FEET

OF

MY BELOVED LORD OF
UNFATHOMABLE GLORY

BHAGAVAN SRI SATHYA SAI BABA

FOREWORD

We can not even begin to gauge the power behind the
THOUSAND NAMES OF LORD VISHNU.
Mysterious are the workings of the impact of these
Sacred Names upon our being.
Thirsting souls eagerly reach out for this Nectar Supreme.
In my zest to imbibe ever deeper the Divine Names of
Lord Vishnu - I made a humble attempt to contemplate on each
one in order to carry Its tune a little further into my consciousness
and out of this effort came into being these

THOUSAND SONGS OF LORD VISHNU.

The author.

INTRODUCTION

The Thousand Names of Lord Vishnu are a part of the well-known epic the Mahabharata. They form the answer to a question posed by King Yuddhisthira to Bhisma, the son of Santanu. The question was

..“Who in this universe is the one Lord,
the One in Whom all should seek refuge,
the One by Whom glorifying and praising one attains perfection?
Which road do you consider the Royal Road leading to salvation?
What is it that we should chant and recite in order to find freedom from this cycle of birth and death? ..

Bhisma responded:

..“Glorifying the All-pervading Lord by these Thousand Names, contemplating on Him, Lord Vishnu, the Lord of all Lords, the Supreme Spirit, the Ultimate Authority of all Creation, the One Who is without beginning and without end, such an earnest worshiper, who repeatedly bows to the Absolute Being will undoubtedly be free from all sorrows and afflictions.

The Royal Road to liberation consist of always praising with sweet devotion the One Who has Lotus-like Eyes, the Author of the Vedas, the Truth Absolute, the Designer of the Universe, the Essence of all Beings, the One Whose Grace enhances the glory of the people.

In order to discard all accumulated sins and nourished fears - listen to the Thousand Names of Lord Vishnu, the Lord of the Universe, the Supreme Source of all Auspiciousness, the Father of all Creation from Whom all beings emerge at the dawn of creation and into Whom all beings dissolve at the end of the cycle of Time. For the welfare of all - I shall recite to you the Glorious Names of Lord Vishnu, which express His attributes that are sung by the sages”..

I seek in all earnestness the Grace of our Lord Divine that He may bestow the same profound blessings upon those who delve with devotion into these Thousand Songs of Lord Vishnu.

O LORD - I PRAY
THAT HEREBY THE MYSTERY OF YOUR GLORY
MAY PENETRATE DEEP INTO THE AWARENESS
OF OUR HEART, MIND AND SOUL.

THE THOUSAND SONGS OF LORD VISHNU

1. I bow to the LORD
   Who constitute the UNIVERSE
   O Lord Divine, Your Embodiment is the Universe
   I do not have to look far to find You
   I am surrounded by Your Magnitude
   and mesmerized by the unfailing laws of perfection
   which sustain this Universe
   Accept, my love, Oh Perfect One

2. I bow to the LORD
   Who is ALL-PERVADING
   Your Breath Divine makes the eye to see
   and the ears to hear
   It invites dull matter to succumb to the Dance of Life
   and effortlessly glorifies Your Nature

3. I bow to the LORD
   Who is YAJNA
   The Essence of Sacrifices
   My Lord, Who invented Sacrifice
   Who enjoys the Sacrifice
   Who sacrifices
   Who instills the Joy of Sacrifice into the sacrificer
   Sublime is my Lord of Sacrifices

4. I bow to the LORD
   Who is the LORD OF PAST, PRESENT AND FUTURE
   The spell of Your Maya fragments the Flow Eternal
   and playfully You tie us by the Cord of Time
   so, that obey Your Law of Karma
   in which You lay bare the display of Justice

5. I bow to the LORD
Who is the CREATOR OF BEINGS
Endless is Your Power
for infinite is Your Creation of multitudinous beings
I adore You, Oh Lord
from Whose Fire has emanated
countless flames and sparkles

6. I bow to the LORD
Who is the NOURISHER OF BEINGS
The Sustainer of all life
The Essence of all beings
The Mother of all children
The Provider for all needs
You are the All for all at all times

7. I bow to the LORD
Who is PURE EXISTENCE
Who withdraws all polarities
Who exudes Oneness
yet rests in perfect peace
on the Ocean of Sacred Stillness

8. I bow to the LORD
Who is the SELF OF ALL BEINGS
Who shines through the shattered minds
dwells in the contemplation
of His unruffled Nature Divine
and His Bliss soothes our agony

9. I bow to the LORD
Who is the CAUSE OF ALL BEINGS
Who with great joy invested Lord Brahma with the power to create the worlds
to bring motion where there is stillness
to make active what is inactive
And glorious became all Manifestations

10. **I bow to the LORD**
Who is PURE ESSENCE
The Only Substance of Life
The Embodiment of Supreme Reality
Your Majesty stands untouched
You Glory unmatched

11. **I bow to the LORD**
Who is the SUPREME SPIRIT
The One to Whom all gods pay homage
The One to Whom all yogis aspire to
The One to Whom all creatures pray and
seek your blessings
The only One Who bestows Grace upon
the humble ones
Such is my Lord, the Supreme Spirit

12. **I bow to the LORD**
Who is the SUPREME GOAL
The Liberator of imprisoned souls
Your Sight heralds the moment of Freedom
that our tears of joy will cleanse our worldly vision
as we prostrate at Your Lotus Feet

13. **I bow to the LORD**
Who is IMMUTABLE
You are the blank slate on which mankind
busily scribbles its imagined notions
You are the ever reigning silence
while at the core of all sound
Forever unchanging in an ever changing world

14. **I bow to the LORD**
Who is the PRIMEVAL PERSON
The Cause of all effects
You are the One Who rests on the Ocean of Milk
The Sea of Contentment
where all manifestations were born
and from where all creation shall withdraw

15. I bow to the LORD
Who is the WITNESS OF JOY AND SORROW
O Lord, You are like the Sun
showering Your Rays of Love
on saints and sinners alike
Always undisturbed
Always undiminished

16. I bow to the LORD
Who is the KNOWER-OF-THE-FIELD
The Indweller in this labyrinth of flesh and bones
The Architect of these veins and arteries
The Composer of the melody
of the mind, heart and soul

17. I bow to the LORD
Who is INDESTRUCTIBLE
His Splendor is vast
His Glory is unsurpassed
His Power is unobstructed
He remains indestructible

18. I bow to the LORD
Who is ATTAINABLE THROUGH YOGA
You are the One moved by pure devotion
Your Heart melts when work transforms into worship
Your Presence waits patiently upon those
who seek You through earnest inquiry

19. I bow to the LORD
Who is the GUIDE OF YOGIS
Who out of sheer compassion
merged out of the Formless
in order to take Form
and bring Home His thirsting souls

20. I bow to the LORD
Who is the LORD OF MAYA AND JIVA
O Lord You playfully draped
the veil of Illusion over Your Doership
and thereby created a multitude of individual 'doers'
so You could love creation infinitely

21. I bow to the LORD
Who is the NARASIMHA INCARNATION
You appeared at the request of the pure-hearted
Prahlada and manifested Yourself in the fearful,
majestic Form of the Man-Lion
in order to slay his father Hiranyakasipu
and free Your beloved devotee Prahlada
from the clutches of unrighteousness

22. I bow to the LORD
Who is the LORD OF LAKSHMI
Our Goddess of Wealth sits always at Your Feet
those who follow You, O Lord
are naturally embraced by Her Divine Presence
bestowing upon them spiritual wealth and glory

23. I bow to the LORD
Who is KESAVA
The sublime Trinity of Brahma, Vishnu and Siva
The Unity from Which flows
creation, sustenance and destruction
in perfect effortless harmony

24. I bow to the LORD
Who is the SUPREME PURUSHA
The Eternal Spirit
silently dwelling in perfect bliss
Motionless holding captive all motion
Effortless embracing all attributes
Glory to the Glorious One

25. I bow to the LORD
Who is the ESSENCE OF ALL
The unchanging substance of all
that is created
The One Who is present outside
as well as inside
Omnipresent is He

26. I bow to the LORD
Who is the AUSPICIOUS ONE
The One Who is capable of bestowing
silence upon the weary minds
Who steeps the longing heart in splendid awe
Who bathes His children in His Golden Love

27. I bow to the LORD
Who is the PURE ONE
Forever unblemished
Radiant with Glory Supreme
Always untarnished
Dazzling with Splendor Divine

28. I bow to the LORD
Who is the PILLAR
O Lord, You are the Sole Support
of this mansion called the world
You are the strength that upholds its formation
Without You - all crumbles

29. I bow to the LORD
Who is the CAUSE OF THE ELEMENTS
From Your Breath Divine the Earth sprung forth
Your Smile so sweet caused Water to flow
Your Dance of Joy sparkled Fire into existence
Your blissful Glance created waves of Air
and Your Song Supreme manifested Ether
so it would carry Its Sacred Sound

30. I bow to the LORD
Who is the IMPERISHABLE TREASURE
You are the Gift Divine for the downtrodden
You are the Wishfulfilling Tree for
all seekers of the Divine
You are the infinite source of Bliss
for the inhabitants of Vaikuntha

31. I bow to the LORD
Who constitutes the MANIFESTATION
The sole cause of the Formless taking Form
The Supreme Spirit evolving nature
and infinity hiding in Time
Mysterious is Your Manifestation

32. I bow to the LORD
Who is the GIVER OF BOONS
Soft is Your Heart, for It melts at
the slightest thought of You
and supremely generous You bestow
impatiently a thousand rewards upon
the humble servant

33. I bow to the LORD
Who is the GOVERNOR
The Absolute Ruler of His borderless territory
The stern Master Who meticulously oversees His Land
and the powerful Protector of its inhabitants

34. I bow to the LORD
Who is the SOURCE OF THE FIVE ELEMENTS
From the Altar of Your Heart
flow the sacred rivers of the senses
carrying Your Substance to all corners
to be enjoyed by You
to be witnessed by You
to be withdrawn by You

35. I bow to the LORD
Who is THE LORD
Overlord of all Lords
Master of Lordship
The One Supreme Lord to
Whom all creation bows

36. I bow to the LORD
Who is the ALMIGHTY
The Fountainhead of Omnipresence
The Source of Omnipotence
The Essence of Omniscience
Glory to the One Who is All

37. I bow to the LORD
Who is the SELF-BORN
No one preceded Him
No one conceived Him
Eternal is His Presence
Infinite His Existence

38. I bow to the LORD
Who is the BESTOWER OF AUSPICIOUSNESS
The Grantor of Glory
The Inspirer of Awe
The Distributor of Splendor
The Invoker of Knowledge Supreme

39. I bow to the LORD
Who is the SUN
Your Existence lends us life
Your Brilliance absorbs the world's gloom
Your Heat evaporates the impurities of this Age
Your Love relentlessly scorches our beings

40. I bow to the LORD
Who has LOTUS-LIKE EYES
Your Eyelids are like the petals
that open up to the silent glory
of the Lotus of Love
and we are invited to drink
of this Fountain of Radiance Divine

41. I bow to the LORD
Whose Breath is the VEDAS
That which emanates from Your Being
becomes the Shower of Grace,
the Treasure Cove for all seekers,
the Remedy for all that ails

42. I bow to the LORD
Who is the CHANGELESS
The Embodiment of perfect equanimity
Never swayed by waves of opposites
Never moved by moods of different colors
Always steadfast
Always there - always here

43. I bow to the LORD
Who is the SUBSTRATUM
The uncreated Creation
The unmanifested Manifestation
The inactive Action
The formless Formation of All that is

44. I bow to the LORD
Who is the DISPENSER OF LAWS
His Authority governs the course of unbending rules
and assures that justice prevails
All causes will meet their effects
All doings will find their consequences

45. I bow to the LORD
Who is the SUBTLEST SUPPORTER
The invisible Thread that upholds
the Cloth of the Universe
You are the Singer of Silence
lending music to every song
and dance to all motion

46. I bow to the LORD
Who is the INDEFINABLE
Your Glory is impenetrable
Your Vastness escapes our hasty expressions
Your Divinity eludes our most earnest inquiry
and smilingly You remain unconquerable

47. I bow to the LORD
Who is HRISHIKESA
The Absolute Master of the Senses
The Director of the Play
between the object, the organ and the perception
and the Inspirer of their Dance

48. I bow to the LORD
Who is PADMANABHA
Creation sprang forth from
the Golden Lotus emanating from Your Navel
lending Superb Charm to the Eternal One

49. I bow to the LORD
Who is the LORD OF IMMORTALS
Endlessly surrounded by those
who know no other than He
Constantly praised by those
who have conquered Time
Beginninglessly embraced by those
of pure devotion

50. I bow to the LORD
Who is the CREATOR
You are the Designer of the Universe
The One Who decided to become the many
in order to multiply Love by Love
so all could see Love

51. I bow to the LORD
Who is the MANTRA
The Wisdom of Words
clothed in majestic melody,
that pierce through dullness
into the Realm of Absolute Truth

52. I bow to the LORD
Who is the FOUNDER
You are the One Who brings dissolution
to this Universe
You are the Annihilator of all
that claims existence
You are the Fire which reduces
everything to ashes

53. I bow to the LORD
Who is the SUPREMELY GROSS
Your Form is the Universe
Your Breath is Its Vastness
Your Smile adorns the sky with
the million sparkles of Stars

54. I bow to the LORD
Who is ANCIENT AND MOTIONLESS
You are the Oldest of the old
in Whom Time does not count
You are the Essence of motion
in Whom action does not take place

55. I bow to the LORD
Who is IMPERCEPTIBLE
Endlessly intriguing is the quest
for finding Your Truth
Forever unfruitful its noble effort
O Divine Master of Elusiveness
we shall seek You unceasingly

56. I bow to the LORD
Who is PERMANENT
Anything temporary cannot gauge
the depth of Permanence
It can only succumb to its fathomless horizon
and surrender its every breath
in perfect faith to this Master Supreme

57. I bow to the LORD
Who is LORD KRISHNA
The Avatar Par Excellence
The playful Cowherdboy of Brindavan
The soul-ravishing Enchanter of the Gopis
The proud Player of the Flute

58. I bow to the LORD
Who is RED-EYED
He is blue-colored
clothed in yellow
wears a Crown and
is adorned with a Garland of Flowers
Beauty Incarnate

59. I bow to the LORD
Who is the SUPREME DESTROYER
You extinguish the Fire Which brought Life
You pulverize all that assumed form
You nullify everything that calculated Time
The Many - once again - fold back into the One

60. I bow to the LORD
Who is the PERFECT
Superb is the Manifest
Sublime is the Unmanifest
Supreme is the Lord of both
Unfathomable is His Glory

61. I bow to the LORD
Who is the SUPPORTER OF THE THREE QUARTERS
Your Smile reigns in the region above
Your Frown clouds the sky of the lower region
and Your watchful Eye keeps track of the actions in the middle region
Your Law prevails

62. I bow to the LORD
Who is the PURIFIER
Who makes shine dull-minded matter
Who wipes clean the imagined dirt
Who transforms poison into nectar
Inconceivable is His Grace

63. I bow to the LORD
Who is SUPREME CONSCIOUSNESS
Your Presence sweeps away all notions
Your Glory absorbs all judgments
Your Majesty sets ablaze the latent Spark Divine
and we become engulfed in Your Fire of Love

64. I bow to the LORD
Who is the ADMINISTRATOR
The scrupulous law-maker
of the microscopic world
as well as the macroscopic universe
And all have to salute Your Sovereignty

65. I bow to the LORD
Who is the SOURCE OF LIFE
O Fountain of Fluid Gold
Your Golden Flow of Nectar
ignites the life in our souls
and in gratitude we dance to
Your Song of Joyous Creation

66. I bow to the LORD
Who is the SUSTAINER
The One Whose Breath
changes the inanimate to the animate
The One Whose Glance
makes conscious the unconscious
Sacred is His Will

67. I bow to the LORD
Who is the ELDEST
Where Time is counted
You are called the Ancient One
for no one knows the beginning
of Your Glorious Being
for in our bafflement the concept of infinity escapes

68. I bow to the LORD
Who is MOST GLORIOUS
We contemplate Your Radiance Divine
and we become submerged in Your Light of Love
Superbly gentle is Your Glory
yet unmercifully all-consuming

69. I bow to the LORD
Who is the CREATOR
Manifold is Your Offspring
Magnificent is Your Mastery
Mesmerizing Your Will for Creation
forever awe-inspiring

70. I bow to the LORD
Who is the WOMB OF THE WORLD
Indisputable You are One
in Whom a second does not exist
The phantom Multitudes whirl wearily in Your Womb
busily creating their worlds

71. I bow to the LORD
Who is the PROTECTOR OF THE EARTH
Your watchful Eye whisks away all discomfort
Your Motherly Embrace soothes the agony
of those whose hands are folded in reverence
and whose eyes are always turned upwards
Your ever-ready Grace melts my heart

72. I bow to the LORD
Who is the SILENT WITNESS
In the very depth of silence
withdrawn from all actions
we catch a glimpse of the Splendid One
spreading His benevolent Gaze
over our contemplative souls

73. I bow to the LORD
Who is the DESTROYER OF VAASANAS
Eager to protect
You are quick to destroy the demons
when Your Presence is noted
and efficient is Your scorching Fire

74. I bow to the LORD
Who is OMNIPOTENT
All-powerful
Perpetually present
Fully independent
Completely self-sufficient

75. **I bow to the LORD**
Who is COURAGEOUS
Intriguing is Your Fearlessness
It is Sacred Food to the frightened soul
It lifts up the feeble notions of existence
and allows Self-effulgence to emerge

76. **I bow to the LORD**
Who is the WIELDER OF THE BOW
As Lord Rama with Your Bow and Arrow
You portray an ever-present preparedness
to maintain peace and order
And make those who adore You feel safe

77. **I bow to the LORD**
Who is SUPREMELY INTELLIGENT
The source of all intelligence
finds its origin in Your Intellect
and gracefully submits to Its unquestionable Authority
Limitless is Its profound impact

78. **I bow to the LORD**
Who is VAAMANA
As the incarnation of the Divine Dwarf
He took three pieces of land
from King Bali and
sealed this conquest of the three spheres of the King
by placing His Divine Foot upon his head
Victorious and free became King Bali

79. **I bow to the LORD**
Who is ALL-PERVADING
There is no place where You are not
There is no form which is not Yours
There is no name which does not denote You
There is none other than You

80. I bow to the LORD
Who is UNEQUALLED
Formidable is Your Prowess
Inconceivable the extent of Your Expanse
Unfathomable the intent of Your Divine Will
Incomprehensible the depth of Your Grace

81. I bow to the LORD
Who is ALL-POWERFUL
Immeasurable is Your Strength
Unconquerable is Your Valor
You are the very source of Strength and Power
All-mighty is Your Nature Divine

82. I bow to the LORD
Who is the KNOWER
The Inhabitant of my heart, mind and soul
The Witness to my feelings, thoughts and emotions
My closest Friend
My nearest Relative
It is He Who is mySelf

83. I bow to the LORD
Who is the REWARDER OF ACTION
You are the Instiller of all action
and the One Who anticipates its reward
You design, play and witness
the Show of Your Maya
Inscrutable are Your Workings

84. I bow to the LORD
Who is SELF-ESTABLISHED
Fully sufficient in His Own Self is He
Dwelling blissfully in His Consciousness
Ever pervaded by His Truth Divine
He finds no other support than Himself

85. **I bow to the LORD**
Who is the GOD OF GODS
The sovereign Lord of all Lords
The Dust of Your Feet
is carried reverentially on
the heads of the greatest gods in all heavens

86. **I bow to the LORD**
Who is REFUGE
O Lord - there is no other Shelter than You
The mere utterance of Your Name
provides us with a shield of protection
The adoration of Your Feet
assures us the loving embrace of Your Grace

87. **I bow to the LORD**
Who is INFINITE BLISS
You are the One
Who perceives no other
Love reflecting Love
Love absorbing Love
Timeless Bliss

88. **I bow to the LORD**
Who is the SEED OF THE WORLD
You are the unmanifest Self
where all manifestations rest
and at Your Command all worlds emerge
All beings, all forms sprout forth
from Your Creative Thought

89. **I bow to the LORD**
Who is the SOURCE OF ALL BEINGS
The Supreme Birth of all Existence
finds its origin in You
and none can comprehend
the majestic power that lies
behind this Creation of Wonder

90. I bow to the LORD
Who is EFFULGENT
What greater beauty is there
than the Lustre of Radiance Divine?
Awe-inspiring is His Infinite Aura
Forever luminous - wholly pervading

91. I bow to the LORD
Who is the LORD OF TIME
Time-bound limits are Your sweet temptations
for the fascination of the worldly-minded
But each segment of Time
is a fraction of Your Infinity
Therefore Time is Your Form

92. I bow to the LORD
Who is UNAPPROACHABLE
The ignorance of darkness
flees from Your effulgent Being
Unable to approach You
all notions have to disperse
and in humble reverence
we prostrate at Your Lotus Feet

93. I bow to the LORD
Who is PURE KNOWLEDGE
Knowledge Supreme is the natural outflow
from Your Divine Consciousness
and gracefully It embraces and
pervades the Creation of all Worlds
Superbly efficient in Its Expression

94. I bow to the LORD
Who is ALL-SEEING
He plays everywhere
He dwells in everything
He expresses Himself in everyone
Inescapable is His Glance

95. **I bow to the LORD**
Who is UNBORN
Without origin
Without source
Without birth
Such is the Nature of our Lord Divine

96. **I bow to the LORD**
Who is the ALMIGHTY
Nothing excels Him
Nobody surpasses Him
Everything salutes Him
Everybody bows down to the Immortal One

97. **I bow to the LORD**
Who is ESTABLISHED
Steeped in Your own Glory
His solely on His Effulgence
and rests perfectly within Himself
This is His only Support

98. **I bow to the LORD**
Who is FINAL BEATITUDE
O how sweet is our glorious destination
Our merging in Your Effulgence
marks the longed for Blessed Victory
All endeavors are rewarded

99. **I bow to the LORD**
Who is the PRIMARY CAUSE
From Whom Time emanated
and out of Time all elements came into being
and showered the world
with their mesmerizing play of Illusion
Dazzling is Your Expression

100. I bow to the LORD
Who is EVER PURE
Untainted is Your Nature
Forever auspicious
Undiminishing in Its Power
Incapable of comprehension

101. I bow to the LORD
Who is the GREAT BOAR
During the incarnation of the Great Boar Varaha
You uplifted the Earth in order
to save it from the waters of dissolution
and thereby displayed
the execution of Dharma

102. I bow to the LORD
Who has INFINITE FORMS
Incalculable are Your Manifestations
Limitless the extent of Your Expressions
You shine forth in every Name and Form
For all dwell within Your Being

103. I bow to the LORD
Who is the LIBERATED
Always free
No bondage mars Your Majesty
None can captivate You
Nothing limits You

104. I bow to the LORD
Who is the ESSENCE OF THE ELEMENTS
As the Ultimate Source of the Elements
You pervade all that is built up
by the five elements
You are their Cause, their Modification, their Effects

105. I bow to the LORD
Who is SUPREMELY PURE-MINDED
Effulgent is His resplendent Mind
It beholds all Existence
Its Thought carries the Universe
Its Joy creates Men

106. I bow to the LORD
Who is TRUTH
Truth has no other support than You
The four Pillars of Your Mansion
are Your four gracious Arms
Your Roof is formed by Your Crown
Your Foundation is the Golden Lotus

107. I bow to the LORD
Who is COMMENSURATE IN ALL
No one is superior to another
No one is inferior to another
For You are in all
and the thought of comparison
does not arise in You

108. I bow to the LORD
Who is ACCEPTABLE
Your Presence in all
invokes acceptance for all
You can not be limited by
the foolishness of favorable or unfavorable thoughts
Your August Presence far exceeds these shortcomings

109. I bow to the LORD
Who is EQUAL
No rise, no fall
No storm, no calm
Perfect equanimity
Balance personified

110. I bow to the LORD
Who is EVER USEFUL
No praise is cast to the wind
No worship will go in vain
No tears of Love will fall upon barren ground
For He consumes all with great fervor
and His Gratitude enraptures us with Divine Bliss

111. I bow to the LORD
Who is the DWELLER IN THE HEART CAVE
Nestled in the abode of our hearts
You wait patiently in hiding
until we find and realize
the Golden Lotus our hearts offer

112. I bow to the LORD
Who is DHARMIC KARMA
All Your Actions excel in virtuous conduct
Always in tune with the rules
You prescribed for each stage in life
A beautiful display of executing Duty Divine

113. I bow to the LORD
Who is DHARMIC FORM
For the sake of upholding Dharma
and restoring righteousness
You take Form from time to time
and bless this dry Earth
with Your Shower of Nectarine Grace

114. I bow to the LORD
Who is the LIQUIDATOR OF ALL SORROWS
The One Who destroys all worries
The One Who absorbs all anxieties
The One Who transforms fear into faith
and tears into joy
Unbounded Grace

115. I bow to the LORD
Who is of MANY HEADS
O Lord of Thousand Heads
Your Forms are countless
All Forms are Yours
All Manifestations are Your Expressions
The Multitudes - All are One in You

116. I bow to the LORD
Who is KING
Unquestionable is Your Authority
Immovable Your Will
Your Protection all-embracing
O Lordly King Your Reign is Golden

117. I bow to the LORD
Who is the TOTAL CAUSE OF THE UNIVERSE
The Supreme Cause
The only Reason for the Manifestation
The One Who created the Thought of Creation
The Father of the Universe

118. I bow to the LORD
Who is of DIVINE NAMES
Unequalled is the Supreme Nectar
Which nourishes us through the hearing
and reading of Your Divine Names
Sweet devotion effortlessly sprouts forth
from this glorious occupation
Mysterious are the workings of Your Grace

119. I bow to the LORD
Who is IMMORTAL
Ageless is He
Undying is His Nature
Perpetual His Glory
Deathless, birthless
Infinite Existence

120. I bow to the LORD
Who is CHANGELESS
No ripple can be found on
the Lake of His Divine Mind
No stirring can be caused
upon the Permanent Field of His Supreme Energy

121. I bow to the LORD
Who is the GLORIOUS DESTINATION
You are the Sacred Fire of Love
Which ignites our small sparkles
into majestic flames of Truth
to be forever engulfed by Your Glory

122. I bow to the LORD
Who is of GREAT TAPAS
His Austerity gives rise to
the Supreme Knowledge Absolute
and expresses Itself effortlessly in
Omnipotence, Omniscience and Omnipresence
We salute the Splendid One

123. I bow to the LORD
Who is ALL-PERVADING
Only You are everywhere
No segments, no fractions
Eternally Here
Forever Now
O, ceaseless Flow Divine, we adore You

124. I bow to the LORD
Who is EFFULGENT AND OMNISCIENT
Your Radiance exceeds the horizon
You illumine Illumination
Your Wisdom creates Knowledge
All-powerful, ever-present

125. I bow to the LORD
Who is the ALMIGHTY
All demons flee before Your terrifying Might
Threatening their very existence by
Your piercing Glance they disperse
Slaying the Evil and protecting the Good
this is the Might of our Lord

126. I bow to the LORD
Who is the BESTOWER OF JOYS
No prayer remains unanswered
Its manifestation far exceeds our imagination
You transform temporary joys
into an unceasing Flow of Nectar Divine
And blissfully we partake of Your Gift

127. I bow to the LORD
Who is the VEDAS
Your Sacred Scriptures offer us
the Lamp of Your Light
the Wisdom of Your Truth
the Nectar of Your Knowledge

128. I bow to the LORD
Who is the KNOWER OF THE VEDAS
The Teacher of the Vedas
The Author of Sacred Scriptures
The Instructor of Wisdom Divine
The Source of All Knowledge

129. I bow to the LORD
Who is ALL-PERFECT
Who is Complete in every aspect
Who is Self-fulfilled
Without defects
Purity personified

130. I bow to the LORD
Whose LIMBS ARE THE VEDAS
Your Cosmic Being, out of sheer compassion,
sprouts forth into various limbs
Spreading Your infinite Love
Carrying Your Message of Wisdom

131. I bow to the LORD
Who is the CONTEMPLATOR OF THE VEDAS
Your Contemplation on the Sacred Scriptures
lends the Supreme Glory to Its Aura
Your penetrating Glance suffuses Its Words
with Knowledge of the Absolute

132. I bow to the LORD
Who is the SEER
You are the One
for Whom there are no secrets
The One, Whose Eyes never close
Your Glance sustains creation

133. I bow to the LORD
Who is the CHIEF OF THE PEOPLE
As the Ultimate Ruler of all
You witness this Universe
and Your Divine Leadership
holds the Manifest in check

134. I bow to the LORD
Who is the CHIEF OF THE GODS
There is no greater God
There is no higher Deity
There is no one more Splendid
There is none more Powerful
Superior is my Lord of Lords

135. I bow to the LORD
Who is the OVERSEER OF DHARMA
You are the Holder of the Scale
which tells of the merits and demerits
accumulated by our wandering souls
and in accordance You shower blessings
or awaken us by inducing hardships

136. I bow to the LORD
Who is the CREATED-CREATOR
You embody the Totality of the Universe
for You are the Manifested - as the effect
of Your Unmanifested Self
The First Cause of Creation

137. I bow to the LORD
Who is the FOUR-FOLD SELF
You evolve the four states of the mind
In the waking hours You predominate as action
In the dream state You play out the workings of the mind
In deep sleep You invoke rest
In Awareness Your Grace makes us the Witness

138. I bow to the LORD
Who is the FOUR-FOLD MANIFESTATIONS
As Vasudeva You preside over Reason
The Manifestation of Sankarasana rules the Ego
Pradyumna governs the Intellect
and Aniruddha holds sway over the mind

139. I bow to the LORD
Who is FOUR-TEETHED
Grand was Your Manifestation
as Narasimha, the Man-Lion,
endowed with four formidable fangs
in order to strike terror
in the hearts of the evil ones

140. I bow to the LORD
Who is FOUR-ARMED
Your Sublime Form is adorned
with Four gracious Arms
carrying Your Message of Truth
in the Form of the Conch,
the Mace, the Discus and the Lotus

141. I bow to the LORD
Who is SELF-EFFULGENT
Filled with Light is HE
Surrounded by Light
Spreading Light
Manifesting Light
My Lord is the Light of all Light

142. I bow to the LORD
Who is FOOD
He is the Enjoyer of that
which is consumed by the senses
for He witnesses Himself
in the very object attracted by the senses

143. I bow to the LORD
Who is the EXPERIENCER
Only He experiences
for there is no other Entity
He creates, enjoys
absorbs and rests

144. I bow to the LORD
Who is the FORGIVER
In Your vast Goodness
You quickly suppress the bad
and infinitely emphasize the good
Always inspiring the Vision of Love

145. I bow to the LORD
Who is the CREATOR
Your Will brought into existence
this bountiful Universe
filled with the glowing Fire of Your Love
carried by Your benevolent Smile

146. I bow to the LORD
Who is UNCONTAMINATED
Without blemish is the Golden One
No impurity can attach to the Lord of Splendor
No shadow covers His Aura
Impeccable is He, our Lord Divine

147. I bow to the LORD
Who is VICTORIOUS
Your Will is invincible
Your Truth forever prevails
Your Mastery unquestioned
Glorious is Your unmatched Victory

148. I bow to the LORD
Who is EVER-SUCCESSFUL
The One, Whose undertakings are triumphant
for Love is His only motive
and Love knows no failure
Love finds Love as Its reward

149. I bow to the LORD
Who is the CAUSE OF THE UNIVERSE
The Source of Love is You, my Lord
The Source of Light is You
The Source of Being is You
You are the all-blissful Source of All This

150. I bow to the LORD
Who is REPEATEDLY-INDWELLING
Time and again You nestle Yourself
within the hearts of beings
sustaining all life with Your Divinity
embracing all with Your Glory

151. I bow to the LORD
Who is UPENDRA
As the Deity Upendra,
the younger brother of Indra,
You preside over the faculty of the feet
and gracefully enable us to visit Holy Places

152. I bow to the LORD
Who is the VAAMANA INCARNATION
The glorious Lustre of the short-statured
Brahmin Boy with His Staff and Kamandalu
outshone all the gathered ones at
King Bali's sacrificial Ceremony

153. I bow to the LORD
Who is LOFTY
His Supreme Height transcends
Earth, Heaven and Sky
and thereby elevates the diminutive
gallantly into His Magnitude

154. I bow to the LORD
Who is PURPOSEFUL
His every Word carries His infinite Message
His every Thought embraces with compassion all that ails
The effect of His every Deed scintillates
through the timeless ages

155. I bow to the LORD
Who is EVER PURE
O How fortunate are the ones
who adore and worship You
Instantly the dross of worldly life
is consumed by Your all-purifying Nature
You are the Embodiment of Grace

156. I bow to the LORD
Who is MIGHTY
Undiminishing in Strength
Infallible in Might
Grand in Splendor
Unequalled in Glory

157. I bow to the LORD
Who is the SOVEREIGN OF INDRA
Indra, the Lord of Paradise,
bows before Him
His Attributes far outshine
the noble qualities of Indra

158. I bow to the LORD
Who is the HOLDER UNTO HIMSELF
He sees all within Himself
He surrounds all by Himsself
He pulls all unto Himself
He, Himself is All

159. I bow to the LORD
Who is CREATION
You alone are responsible for Creation
Playfully the Unmanifest became Manifest
Your Divine Thought brought into existence
the dazzling details of this unity of multitudes

160. I bow to the LORD
Who is the SELF-SUPPORTER
He does not go outside of Himself
He does not reach beyond Himself
for there are no limits to Himself
Wherever He is - He finds Only Himself

161. I bow to the LORD
Who is the APPOINTING AUTHORITY
His Divine Management secures
order in the ruling of the Universe
He appoints the Great Ones
for the various sacred seats of His Holy Government

162. I bow to the LORD
Who is the ADMINISTRATOR
He administers the Laws of Perfection
and oversees their execution from within
Always guiding, always leading
He is the untiring Master

163. I bow to the LORD
Who is the KNOWABLE
Through the Path of Love and Devotion
You become accessible to us
Through Discrimination and Dispassion
You reveal Yourself to us

164. I bow to the LORD
Who is the SUPREME DOCTOR
He is the One
Who contains all Knowledge
The showering of His Divine Wisdom
graciously heals all that ails

165. **I bow to the LORD**
Who is the ETERNAL YOGI
Your contemplation holds the Universe
Your Love creates Infinity
Your Bliss brings Knowledge Absolute
Your Radiance envelops all with Your Aura Divine

166. **I bow to the LORD**
Who is the DESTROYER OF MIGHTY TYRANTS
Relentless is His Power of Destruction
when He seeks to annihilate those
who obstruct the Path of Righteousness
Unfailing is His Purpose

167. **I bow to the LORD**
Who is the LORD OF KNOWLEDGE
Blue-colored is the Depth of His Infinite Knowledge
Of golden hue is Its Radiance
Self-effulgent Its Essence
Its very Nature is the Embodiment
of our beloved Lord Divine

168. **I bow to the LORD**
Who is of NECTARINE BLISS
O, Giver Supreme, sweeter than sweet
are Your Gifts of Eternity
Anxious, like the loving Mother
You shower Your servant with heavenly Bliss

169. **I bow to the LORD**
Who is BEYOND THE SENSES
Senseless is the effort
to reach the Lord Divine
through the contact of the senses
His realm vastly outgrows their finitude

170. I bow to the LORD
Who is the SUPREME MASTER OF MAYA
With Maya as Your Toy
You joyously create veils
behind which You watch and witness
the maddening foolishness of man's pride

171. I bow to the LORD
Who is the ENTHUSIASTIC ACCOMPLISHER
He is the One, Who
without end, is ever engaged
in the workings of the process of Creation
and fully content, fulfills His Duty Divine

172. I bow to the LORD
Who is OMNIPOTENT
Among the strong ones
He is the Strongest
Among the great ones
He is the Greatest
All-powerful is He

173. I bow to the LORD
Who is OMNISCIENT
He is the Incarnation
of Wisdom Divine
Whose Heart ever contains all Glory
of the Absolute Knowledge

174. I bow to the LORD
Who is SUPREME QUINTESSENCE
Holding the Essence of all existence
within Your Divine Mind
You are the Supreme Master
The Director of Darkness and Light

175. I bow to the LORD
Who is ALL-POWERFUL
Your Being emanates the
silent steady Flow of Strength
Never hesitant, ever full
Undiminishing, ever present

176. I bow to the LORD
Who is SELF-EFFULGENT
Glorious is Your Shine
It absorbs all gloom
and makes the non-existent
merge into the All-Existent Lustre
of Your Brilliance

177. I bow to the LORD
Who is of INTELLIGENT FORM
No recognizable form can
be denoted as being Him
He is imperceptible through
the function of the senses

178. I bow to the LORD
Who is GLORIOUS
Your Golden Glory envelops
all Your Doings and
Supreme Greatness exudes
from Your Divine Actions

179. I bow to the LORD
Who is INESTIMABLE
You are beyond measure
You are beyond estimation
No calculation can sum up
the Totality of Your Glorious Being

180. I bow to the LORD

Who is the SUPPORTER OF THE MOUNTAIN
Our minds feast endlessly
upon the events of Your Divine Incarnations
Our souls are rapt in awe
when the sacred story of Lord Krishna
supporting the Govardhana Mountain, is recalled

181. I bow to the LORD

Who is the WIELDER OF THE GREAT BOW
Always ready to exercise Your Might
over the unrighteous ones
You are called the Wielder of the Bow
displaying the Splendor of Justice

182. I bow to the LORD

Who is the SUPPORTER OF THE EARTH
During the Times of Dissolution
when all is submerged by water
You graciously held up the Earth
O Master of Fate

183. I bow to the LORD

Who is the ABODE OF LAKSHMI
Nestled upon Your Chest
Goddess Lakshmi dwells eternally
Always worshipping You
Forever serving You

184. I bow to the LORD

Who is the GOAL OF THE VIRTUOUS
The Highest Blessing is Your Gift
You grant the Ultimate Goal
You open the Final Door for
those who have become truly humble

185. I bow to the LORD
Who is IRRESISTIBLE
Irresistible is Your Power
Obstructions cannot be made
by any one or anything when
You desire to execute Your Will

186. I bow to the LORD
Who is the ENCHANTER OF THE GODS
You are the Delighter Supreme
for all greater and lesser Deities
Your Melody Divine enraptures
their pure souls and in wondrous Bliss
they perform their designated duties

187. I bow to the LORD
Who is the PROTECTOR OF THE COWS
Sacred are the Cows
who have secured Your utmost Care
You are known as the Leader of the Cows
and Govinda is Your Name

188. I bow to the LORD
Who is the LORD OF THE SEERS
He, Who is the Designer
of all Existence and therefore
the One, Who contains all meanings
is Lord of all the Wise Ones

189. I bow to the LORD
Who is LUSTROUS
The glorious Lustre which
shines forth from the Holy Ones
is Your Lustre which
You pour as a Divine Flow of Nectar
into their sacred souls

190. I bow to the LORD
Who is the CONTROLLER
You keep even the scale
of right and wrong doings
and You become the Great Saviour
when darkness threatens the Glow of Light

191. I bow to the LORD
Who AM I
Blesses are those who fully identify
themselves with Your Nature Divine
Their subtle bodies become scorched
by Your Fire - they become One with You

192. I bow to the LORD
Who is of BEAUTIFUL WINGS
The Flight of Divinity is held aloft
by the Wings of Dharma and Adharma
The perfect balance of opposites
is Your secret hiding place

193. I bow to the LORD
Who is ANANTA
The Sacred Serpent Ananta spreads
Its Thousand Hoods in great Splendor
thereby exhibiting Its formidable Strength
Its Power is the Lord's Manifestation

194. I bow to the LORD
Who is the SUPPORTER OF THE CREATOR
Even our Creator, Lord Brahma,
finds His Origin in You, O Lord Supreme
You created Him in order
for Him to create the Worlds

195. I bow to the LORD
Who is of GLORIOUS TAPAS
Deeply mysterious are the effects
of the austerities You perform
during Your many Incarnations
Its Fires purify all regions
and ignite all with Your Glory

196. I bow to the LORD
Who is PADMANAABHA
The Beauty of a Lotus adorns His Navel
resembling the center of the human heart
that Lotus Seat which He loves to occupy
Such is our Lord of the Golden Lotus

197. I bow to the LORD
Who is the LORD OF CREATURES
O how endless are the numbers
of Your created beings
all aspiring after Your loving Care
and graciously You embrace all with Your Love

198. I bow to the LORD
Who is CHANGELESS
Unknown to Him is Death
Unknown to Him are changes
His Nature is limitless
His Being is Permanent

199. I bow to the LORD
Who is the SEER
Everything is known to Him
Not a speck of dust on our souls
escapes His all-seeing Eye
His Glance penetrates through
all of the Universe
Nothing is concealed from Him

200. **I bow to the LORD**
Who is the ANNIHILATOR
As the Lord of Destruction
You absorb all Creation
emphasizing the evanescence
of the finite existence of our worlds

201. **I bow to the LORD**
Who is the CO-RELATOR
To ensure the correct balance
You bind the individual to
the fruits of his actions and
gradually he learns through
this display of cause and effect

202. **I bow to the LORD**
Who is the ENJOYER
You are the Experiencer
of all our doings
All that is perceived, consumed
or brought into action
has only You as the Enjoyer

203. **I bow to the LORD**
Who is CONSISTENT
Constant is Your Being
Of steady flow is Your Love Divine
Your Shower of nectarine Radiance permanent
Unwavering is Your all-embracing Compassion

204. **I bow to the LORD**
Who is the CREATOR
He is the Powerful One
Who holds all strings
He enters our hearts
and directs our lives
Glorious is He

205. I bow to the LORD
Who is INVINCIBLE
Powerless are Your enemies
They remain forever without victories
and their endless defeat
brings You Glories untold

206. I bow to the LORD
Who is the RULER
Your Word Supreme directs all
Your Voice of Wisdom protects us
Your Knowledge Absolute governs us
There is no other Ruler but You

207. I bow to the LORD
Who is the CELEBRITY OF THE VEDAS
Your Divine Essence springs forth
from the Sacred Scriptures
and is clothed in many varied ways
and each so sweet to our ears

208. I bow to the LORD
Who is the DESTROYER OF THE ASURAS
Ruthless You become when
defying the mighty demons
Relentlessly You annihilate them
For Your Glory does not permit
the forces of darkness to prevail

209. I bow to the LORD
Who is the GURU
All Gurus prostrate before Him
He, the Ultimate Guru, shines
as the Only Teacher of
Truth, Love and Knowledge

210. I bow to the LORD
Who is the GREATEST TEACHER
Even the highest Gods in all heavens
derive their Knowledge from Him
There is no one superior to Him
The Highest among the High Ones is He

211. I bow to the LORD
Who is the GOAL
For without Him there is nothing
Without Him we are crippled
Without Him all collapses
He is our Support, He is the Goal

212. I bow to the LORD
Who is the TRUTH
His Enigma is Truth
His Breath exudes Truth
His Motion is the Dance of Truth
This is His Only Existence

213. I bow to the LORD
Who is DYNAMIC TRUTH
The Source of Your Invincibility
is Truth alone
The Essence of Your Omnipotence
has solely Truth as Its Foundation

214. I bow to the LORD
Who is of CLOSED EYES
Breathtaking is Your Form
when steeped in deep contemplation
Your closed Eyes deepen the
Aura of Your Silent Glory
O Lord of Divine Mystery

215. I bow to the LORD
Who is of UNWINKING EYES
Alert to all needs
Awake to keep watch
Keen on serving His Devotees
Our Lord does not sleep

216. I bow to the LORD
Who is the WEARER OF THE GARLAND
He is adorned with the Garland
strung with scented flowers, symbolizing
the subtle aspect of the earthly elements
Their fragrance glorifies Him

217. I bow to the LORD
Who is the SAGACIOUS LORD OF ELOQUENCE
He is the Father of the Word
The Beginning of all Knowledge
His Vision is all-comprehensive
He is Wisdom Incarnate

218. I bow to the LORD
Who is the GUIDE
Leading us through the dark jungle
of the confounding worlds
He brings us to His Land of Light
taking all the earnest ones by His Hand

219. I bow to the LORD
Who is the CHIEF
He is the One to
Whom all submit and
in great reverence bow down
He is the Commander
The One and Only Lord

220. I bow to the LORD
Who is RADIANT
O Lord of Radiance
Your Effulgence drapes us
with Love so sweet
Your Brilliance brings
Supreme Silence and in Joy we bathe

221. I bow to the LORD
Who is the LOGICIAN
The steady path of Logic
paves the way to all Knowledge
You are the Master of Common Sense
Who breaks open the dullness of our minds

222. I bow to the LORD
Who is SUPERINTENDENT
You are the Great Controller
over the making of the worlds
As the Chief Commander
You tower high over all beings
Unapproachable is Your Status

223. I bow to the LORD
Who is the PROMOTER
The giving of Life is
in Your Hands alone
Your very Breath sustains
all forms of Life

224. I bow to the LORD
Who is of INNUMERABLE HEADS
Your Life is all lives
Your Form is all forms
Your Being is all beings
You are the One with countless Heads

225. I bow to the LORD
Who is the SOUL OF THE UNIVERSE
The Center of the Universe is He
The very Hub of the whirling wheel
That sublime Stillness in all motion
there is where we find Him, our Beloved

226. I bow to the LORD
Who is OF INNUMERABLE EYES
He looks through a thousand eyes,
loving His World
He perceives with numerous glances,
enjoying His Creation

227. I bow to the LORD
Who is of INNUMERABLE LEGS
Plentiful are the steps You take
Far and wide are the distances You travel
Yet - You remain motionless
and the horizon is Your Throne

228. I bow to the LORD
Who is of UNSEEN DYNAMISM
He is the One, Who sets in motion
the Grand Wheel of Samsara
and keeps it turning and turning
Powerful is His Intent

229. I bow to the LORD
Who is IMMACULATE
Untarnished by the chains of bondage
Immune to the prison of the senses
Perfectly free is He
Serene and untouched

230. I bow to the LORD
Who is VEILED
Hidden by the dense cloud of thinking
He hides His Rays of Wisdom
and remains unseen by
the struggling soul steeped in ignorance

231. I bow to the LORD
Who is the PROSECUTOR
Intolerable to Him are the ways
of the extroverted and in His Love
He strikes heavy blows in order
for them to turn around and see Him,
the Prosecutor for the sake of Love

232. I bow to the LORD
Who is the SUN
The One, Who manifests Time
He is the Sun, Who regulates
the rhythm of night and day
creating the patterns of our lives

233. I bow to the LORD
Who is FIRE
He is the all-purifying Fire
in Which all is sacrificed
and elevated into the One Source
His Glory - so intense

234. I bow to the LORD
Who is VITAL-AIR
The ever-streaming Flow of Air
constitutes His Residency
The still endless Flow of Infinity
Supreme Light - Supreme Energy

235. I bow to the LORD
Who is the GREAT BOAR
Explicit strength You portrayed
in the Varaaha Incarnation
Taking the Form of the Divine Boar
You supported the Worlds and
thereby instilled feelings of protection

236. I bow to the LORD
Who is of SUPREME GRACE
Supremely merciful is He
Ignoring our faults and shortcomings
He showers us with
His cooling Rain of sweet Nectar
Without hesitation, without distinction

237. I bow to the LORD
Who is the ALL-BLISSFUL SELF
Perpetually emerged in Bliss Divine
You remain steeped in Golden Glory
Abiding in Infinity every moment
You embrace all onto Your Self

238. I bow to the LORD
Who is the SUPPORTER OF THE WORLD
His Strength is the pedestal
on Which the World rests
His Power is the Activator
by Which the World moves

239. I bow to the LORD
Who is the ENJOYER OF THE WORLD
Playfully casting His Net of Maya
over His Creation
He plays all parts and
joyfully enjoys being the Enjoyer

240. **I bow to the LORD**
Who is of MULTITUDINOUS FORMS
You are the One
Who longed to be manifested
into many fragments
You are the Sun
emanating a thousand Rays

241. **I bow to the LORD**
Who is the ADMIRER OF THE RIGHTEOUS
Highly pleased with the virtuous conduct
of the humble ones
He bestows upon them
His all-graceful benevolent Smile

242. **I bow to the LORD**
Who is ADMIRED BY THE RIGHTEOUS
Extolled by the Great Ones
Praised by the Meek Ones
Revered by the noble souls
Our glorious Lord is the Recipient
of all adoration and devotion

243. **I bow to the LORD**
Who is VIRTUOUS
Virtue Incarnate is He
Justice Personified
Displayer of Truth in action
He embodies all-Goodness, and-Righteousness

244. **I bow to the LORD**
Who is the LEADER
Joyfully He gathers His loved ones
for His March of Victories
and fully engaged in spreading His Care
He is the Leader Supreme for all times

245. I bow to the LORD
Who is NARAYANA
O, how beautiful is Your Name
How sweet Its Taste
You are the Supreme Lord
Who resides in all
Who pervades all

246. I bow to the LORD
Who is the GUIDE
The Only Director is He
No power befalls any other
Everything has its essence in Him
All follows Him

247. I bow to the LORD
Who is of INNUMERABLE FORMS
Every name and form belongs to You
No distinction should be made
No differences should be noted
You alone are this Universe

248. I bow to the LORD
Who is the INCOMPREHENSIBLE SELF
Beyond all inquiry is He
Unattainable through reasoning
Mysterious is His Nature
the very Essence of our beings

249. I bow to the LORD
Who is the DISTINGUISHED
Excellence in all qualities
Champion on all fields
Victory in all endeavors
Grand is our Distinguished Lord

250. I bow to the LORD
Who is the PROTECTOR OF THE GOOD
As the Mother of all
You hover over us with gentle care
making sure that no harm will be done
to our helpless souls who seek only You

251. I bow to the LORD
Who is EVER PURE
Flawless is His Nature
Spotless is His immaculate Soul
His Being forever untainted
Perfect is our Golden Lord
Pure in every way

252. I bow to the LORD
Who is ACCOMPLISHED
His Will is the Ultimate Law
nothing remains unfulfilled
when His Divine Thought is directed
towards the desired object

253. I bow to the LORD
Who is of ACCOMPLISHED-WILLING-WISHING
Nothing stands in His Way
His all-powerful Will prevails
and all resolutions shall meet
their accomplishments - because
He knows no obstructions

254. I bow to the LORD
Who is the BESTOWER OF FELICITY
He is the Grantor of Boons
when pleased with sincere effort
He showers His Grace
on the thirsting humble souls

255. **I bow to the LORD**
Who is the MEANS TO BEATITUDE
He is the Doorway to Sacredness
leading us to the Sanctity of His Temple
and in splendorous awe we receive
the Final Deliverance

256. **I bow to the LORD**
Who is the UNIVERSAL ADMINISTRATOR OF DHARMA
Taking in account the performance
of good deeds and spiritual discipline
He distributes evenly
the deserved and longed-for merits

257. **I bow to the LORD**
Who is the SHOWERER OF GRACE
Abundantly generous He graces
His Devotees with all that they aspire for
How sweet is our Lord
for His favorite pastime is the giving of Grace

258. **I bow to the LORD**
Who is VISHNU
Invisibly penetrating All
You pervade Creation
You uphold the Worlds
You sustain the Universe

259. **I bow to the LORD**
Who is the LADDER TO ULTIMATE REALITY
Offering us guidelines for
the different stages in life
He provides liberally the necessary steps
to be taken in order to teach
His Wisdom of Truth

260. I bow to the LORD
Who is the SHOWERING BELLY
Bringing forth countless forms
You are called the Showering Belly
manifesting endless offspring
Creating a myriad of beings

261. I bow to the LORD
Who is the NOURISHER OF ALL
The Blessed Food of Your Grace
elevates us into the higher regions
where our souls are being nourished
by Your ever-loving Care

262. I bow to the LORD
Who is EVER-WAXING
Your Creation is without end
Increasingly multiplying Your Form
through the manifestations of the Universe
You are ever expanding

263. I bow to the LORD
Who is UNAFFECTED
The Supreme Witness is He
Not attached, perfect in balance
Free from grief and pain
within His own Self

264. I bow to the LORD
Who is the REPOSITORY
You contain within Yourself
the contents of all Sacred Scriptures
You are the Fountainhead
of the Holy Stream of Divine Wisdom

265. I bow to the LORD
Who is of GRACEFUL ARMS
Your all-embracing Arms
envelop the Worlds of the Universe
and carry in Motherly Love
her burdens - always protecting
Endless Compassion

266. I bow to the LORD
Who is UNFATHOMABLE
Incapable of grasping Your Glory
We remain at a loss in our awe
Your Splendor cannot be gauged
Your Divine Being remains forever unfathomable

267. I bow to the LORD
Who is ELOQUENT OF HIS GLORY
None can adequately speak of Your Glory
Only Your own Spoken Word
in the form of the Sacred Scriptures
allows us a glimpse of Your Golden Glory

268. I bow to the LORD
Who is the LORD OF INDRA
The King of lordly kings is He
The Supreme Godhead from Whom
emanates the Ultimate Authority
All Gods are His Servants

269. I bow to the LORD
Who is the CONFERER OF PROSPERITY
He is the Bestower of Abundance
Greatly enjoying the role of the Giver
He showers generously the riches
of the outer and inner world

270. **I bow to the LORD**
Who is the INDWELLER
Covering Your Brilliance
like the hidden Diamond
You dwell silently in the enjoyer
as well as in the object of enjoyment
Maya being Your Game

271. **I bow to the LORD**
Who is of INFINITE FORMS
You cannot be captured
in one Form only
Your Divinity demands multiplicity
Therefore - endless are Your Forms

272. **I bow to the LORD**
Who is of UNIVERSAL FORM
Deeply mysterious are Your Forms
since they contain Your Universe
All that was, is and will be
is infinitely present in Your Form

273. **I bow to the LORD**
Who is the PRESIDING DEITY IN THE SUN
O, God of the Sun, I adore You
You warm my heart
with Your comforting Rays
and fill my soul with
the Glow of Your Radiance

274. **I bow to the LORD**
Who is the ILLUMINATOR
Your Light makes vanish
the forces of darkness
Your Brilliance makes effulgent
the dullest layer of worldliness

275. I bow to the LORD
Who is the POSSESSOR OF VIRILITY, BEAUTY AND BRILLIANCE
The Manifestor of Virility
He possesses strength
The Creator of Beauty
He exudes comeliness
The Source of Brilliance
He emanates Radiance

276. I bow to the LORD
Who is the EFFULGENT SELF
In Silence He radiates
like a billion Suns
In this Light Divine
He speaks of Himself and
His Silent Word captivates us

277. I bow to the LORD
Who is the ENLIVENING THERMAL ENERGY
The Love for His World
brought forth the powerful Sun
so we can look up to Her
and in our praise for Her loving Warmth
He sustains the Life in our souls

278. I bow to the LORD
Who is ALL-PROSPEROUS
His Wealth is abundant
His Knowledge is the Source of Infinity
His Righteousness is the Seat of Love Divine
His Compassion is the Fire of His Golden Glory

279. I bow to the LORD
Who is OM
His first Sound enfolds all that is
Its Sacred Vibrations embrace everything
Its Divine Energy echoes through
all manifestations in all worlds

280. I bow to the LORD
Who is MANTRA
Wonderful is the Power
of the Sacred Formula
Its harmonious texture brings forth
the revelation of His Nature

281. I bow to the LORD
Who is the SOOTHING MOONLIGHT
He brings sweet coolness to
our overworked souls
and makes us forget
the hours of worldly struggle

282. I bow to the LORD
Who is RESPLENDENT LIKE THE SUN
There is no likeness to
the Brightness of Your Light
We gaze upon the Sun
in our attempt to come
closer to Your Resplendence

283. I bow to the LORD
Who is the BEGETTER OF THE MOON
He is the One
Who manifested the Moon
The Light of the Night
to soothe our anxious minds
He is our Lord of Compassion

284. I bow to the LORD
Who is SELF-EFFULGENT
Spreading His Glory of Gold
He shines unceasingly
blissfully radiating His Aura Divine
revealing the Beauty of Truth Absolute

285. I bow to the LORD
Who is the MOON
Manifested as the Moon
He is the Caregiver for all
and lovingly sends forth His cooling Rays
to all creation, big and small

286. I bow to the LORD
Who is the LORD OF ALL GODS
His Majesty exudes Supreme Authority
His Divine Splendor commands the Highest Reverence
His all-embracing Love invokes the Sincerest Humility
He is the Lord Absolute

287. I bow to the LORD
Who is DIVINE MEDICINE
He is the One
Who cures the illness of the world
He dissolves in His illuminating Self
the disease of the petty self

288. I bow to the LORD
Who is the BRIDGE TO INFINITE PERFECTION
Our Lord Divine lovingly holds the key
to the highest Temple of Sublime Perfection
He alone is the One
Who carries us into the Light of Divine Love

289. I bow to the LORD
Who is the CHAMPION OF TRUTH AND RIGHTEOUSNESS
His Truth submerges all His workings
into the Ocean of Righteousness
His Righteousness unmistakably conveys
the Message of His Truth

290. **I bow to the LORD**
Who is the LORD OF PAST, PRESENT AND FUTURE
The Timeless One is the genuine Master
over yesterday, today and tomorrow
Time is His Play of Illusion
and we are His subject

291. **I bow to the LORD**
Who is PURIFYING AIR
Like the wind which blows away
the gathered particles of dust
His Presence eliminates promptly
the nurtured notions of the mind

292. **I bow to the LORD**
Who is the SUPREME PURIFIER
Being the Essence of Motion
You embrace all movement
and breathe freely
through the worlds inner and outer

293. **I bow to the LORD**
Who is VITAL AIR
Beginningless, endless, ceaseless
Breath Divine
Flow everlasting
The glorious Substratum for all that is

294. **I bow to the LORD**
Who is the DESTROYER OF DESIRES
His gracious Glance bestows auspiciousness
upon the thirsting souls and
evaporates the dark sways of
the sense-filled mind

295. I bow to the LORD
Who is the FULFILLER OF DESIRES
He is the One
Who knows the innermost secrets
of our hankering hearts
and He takes supreme delight
in the fulfilling of our faintest wishes

296. I bow to the LORD
Who is ABSOLUTE AUSPICIOUS BEAUTY
Unparalleled is the Radiance
of His Supreme Beauty
emphasizing the Sublimity
of His August Auspiciousness

297. I bow to the LORD
Who is the MOST BELOVED
O Lord of Sweetness
Giver of Nectar Divine
Supreme Stealer of our hearts
No one is dearer to us
than Your Effulgent Self

298. I bow to the LORD
Who is the BESTOWER OF DESIRES
Father of instilled wishes
eager to play the loving Mother
to grant their fulfillment
Such is our Lord of Joy

299. I bow to the LORD
Who is the SUPREME LORD
He is the Creator of Excellence
He is the Sustainer of Life Everlasting
He is the Destroyer of fears
His Glory is immeasurable

300. **I bow to the LORD**
Who is the CREATOR OF YUGAS
Instiller of Time
propelling the illusion of change
He creates His Play
of non-existent Existence

301. **I bow to the LORD**
Who is the ADMINISTRATOR OF YUGAS
As the Designer of beginnings and ends
He marks the rhythm of aeons
and folds the web of Time
over His Creation of Mankind

302. **I bow to the LORD**
Who is of INNUMERABLE COSMIC POWERS
Plentiful are the expressions
of His immanent Power
Incomprehensible is the Limitless
to the limited perceiver

303. **I bow to the LORD**
Who is the GREAT SWALLOWER
Eager to retrieve His Manifestation
He calls back Creation
at the end of the Kalpa
and fully satisfied He swallows
all that He expressed

304. **I bow to the LORD**
Who is the IMPERCEPTIBLE
Residing in the Temple of Gold
He remains unobserved
by the mortal eyes turned to
outward views, which pass by
the glorious Vision of His Inner Sanctity

305. **I bow to the LORD**
Who is PERCEPTIBLE
Grace alone opens the door
of His Golden Temple
when He longs for His pure-hearted devotees
to perceive His Glory

306. **I bow to the LORD**
Who is the CONQUEROR OF EVILS
Stampeding the evil tendencies
of the World of Darkness
He initiates the March of Victories
into His Land of Light

307. **I bow to the LORD**
Who is EVER-VICTORIOUS
His Divine Doings constitute
the Dance of Triumph
Ever moving, always elevating
into His Orb of Certainty

308. **I bow to the LORD**
Who is the REPOSITORY OF LOVE
Being the Fountain of Bliss
We long to partake from
the Streams of Your Nectarine Love
O Sustainer of Life Eternal

309. **I bow to the LORD**
Who is the MOST RENOWNED
Known to all
as our innermost Being
We herald Your Presence
as the Temple of the Highest Glory

310. I bow to the LORD
Who is the MOST BELOVED
Profoundly attached to the Glorious One
are the pure-hearted souls
who have discarded all judgments
and regard Him as their Most Beloved

311. I bow to the LORD
Who is the WEARER OF THE PEACOCK FEATHER
Supremely handsome is the Lord of Brindavan
adorned with the peacock feather
He thrills all by His exquisite Sight
what is known to consciousness
gets lost in the rapture of Bliss

312. I bow to the LORD
Who is NAHUSHA
As the Cosmic Player
He veils His children
with the Curtain of Illusion
and allows them to dance
to His Song of Time

313. I bow to the LORD
Who is the INCARNATION OF DHARMA
The Birthplace of all Righteousness
is seated in His Being
His every Act exudes right action
His very Breath holds all Truth

314. I bow to the LORD
Who is the ANNIHILATOR OF ANGER
He eases the stubborn tendencies
of the habitual mind
of those struggling souls, who
in all earnestness seek to praise Him

315. I bow to the LORD
Who is WRATHFUL
There is no limit to His Wrath
when He chooses to destroy
that which resists His Will
Unapproachable is His Might

316. I bow to the LORD
Who is of INFINITE ARMS
Eager to hold His loved ones
He created Himself with innumerable Arms
embracing them tightly
to His loving Heart
He cherishes His own Creation

317. I bow to the LORD
Who is the SUSTAINER OF EARTH
Solely resting upon You
You are Her only Source
The very Essence of her being
Mother Earth sings her praises to You

318. I bow to the LORD
Who is the IMMUTABLE
Immovable in His Essence
Sublimacy in steadfastness
One-pointed in purpose
Equanimity unequalled

319. I bow to the LORD
Who is IMMANENT
The Glorious One, Who contains
all Creation within Him
He is the Only One
worthy of adoration

320. I bow to the LORD
Who is the SUSTAINER
O Giver of Life-Breath
You light the sparkle
of Your Fire Divine in
the hearts and souls of
the multitude of Your created beings

321. I bow to the LORD
Who is the SOURCE OF STRENGTH
Undefeatable are those, who
You have endowed with the prowess
of Your Strength and
victory hails them at all occasions

322. I bow to the LORD
Who is the LORD OF INDRA
As the Incarnation of Vamana
You became the Brother of Indra
Thoroughly enjoying the worldly play of relations
You choose to remain close to Your devotees

323. I bow to the LORD
Who is the OCEAN
Blue-colored, it signifies
His fathomless Depth
Ever-moving, it symbolizes
the Eternal Flow of the Divine

324. I bow to the LORD
Who is the SUBSTRATUM
Anchored in Your Effulgence
in all that exists
Dwelling in Your Glory
is all that will be

325. **I bow to the LORD**
Who is of PERFECT JUDGMENT
No good thought, word or deed
goes unnoticed by the Lord Supreme
and full of eagerness
He rewards those who are deserving

326. **I bow to the LORD**
Who is SELF-SUPPORTER
His Dwelling Place is HimSelf
His Birthplace is HimSelf
His Destination is in Him alone
He is All there IS

327. **I bow to the LORD**
Who is SUBRAMANYA
Infinity Incarnate
Son of Shiva
Man of Perfection
His Expansion embraces the sky

328. **I bow to the LORD**
Who is the UPHOLDER OF DHARMA
He points out the righteous path
He walks the righteous path
He sustains the path of the virtuous
He is the Protector of the Earth

329. **I bow to the LORD**
Who is the SUSTAINER
Pregnant with Creation
He carries all Existence
Beholding with benevolence
the worlds of all times
He is our Creator Supreme

330. I bow to the LORD

Who is the BESTOWER OF BOONS
O Glorious Giver of Nectarine Rain
We refresh ourselves with delight
in Your Shower of Grace
and bow low before Your ever-present Generosity

331. I bow to the LORD

Who is the SUPPORTER OF SEVEN WINDS
As the Master of the Seven Spheres
He whirls the waves of air
and keeps all in motion
as He is pleased with His Creation

332. I bow to the LORD

Who is VAASUDEVA
All-embracing He manifests Himself
in and around all beings
He is the Inspirer from within
He is the Protector from without

333. I bow to the LORD

Who is the SUPREME SUN
Being the Source of all Rays
His Being constitutes the Sun
The Distributor of Warmth
The Emanator of Light

334. I bow to the LORD

Who is the PRIMARY CAUSE
Lord of Devas
God of Angels
King of Men
The Ultimate First

335. I bow to the LORD
Who is the PULVERIZER OF CITIES
At times of dissolution
when the game of illusion
is played out, You simply disintegrate
the phantom bodies of gross,
subtle, and causal matter

336. I bow to the LORD
Who is FREE FROM GRIEF
Unplagued by the six enemies
He remains untouched by modifications
and dwells blissfully
in His Land of Freedom

337. I bow to the LORD
Who ENABLES OTHERS TO CROSS
Mercifully He removes all obstacles
from the struggles of the Truth-seekers
and carries them eagerly to
the other shore of the bewildering ocean

338. I bow to the LORD
Who is the SAVIOUR
Bringing solace to the stressed
He frees the Bound
from the fears of the intimidating world
and celebrates His Grandeur
by saving the fallen ones

339. I bow to the LORD
Who is the VALIANT
Conqueror of Fear
Displayer of undiminishing Courage
He expresses His Truth
of unwavering Perseverance

340. I bow to the LORD
Who is SAURI
Son of Sura
The Divine Offspring of Vasudeva
He is the Glorious Krishna
also known as Sauri

341. I bow to the LORD
Who is the LORD OF ALL CREATURES
Father of all beings
Ruler of all action
Master of creation
You are the Most Beloved of all

342. I bow to the LORD
Who is the ULTIMATE ALLY
The only True Bond we have,
O Lord, is with Your Divine Self
No other relations can reach
into this Sacred Region where
Truth alone remains and
in Joy we unite

343. I bow to the LORD
Who is of INNUMERABLE INCARNATIONS
Lovingly He descends often into His Creation
to be among His loved ones and
to shower His Supreme Grace upon
the ones whom He chooses
to be His contemporaries

344. I bow to the LORD
Who is the BEARER OF LOTUS
Beautifully adorned with the Lotus
He holds out this exquisite Flower
as the beloved promise of the entering
into His Temple of Divine Light

345. I bow to the LORD
Who has EYES LIKE LOTUS PETALS
Indescribable are the Eyes of the Lord
but the desire to express our wonder
never ceases - in our weak utterances
we compare His Divine Eyes with
the petals of the incomparable Lotus

346. I bow to the LORD
Who is LOTUS-NAVELED
As the hub of the whirling Universe
we place Him in our poetry
in the center of the Lotus
Beauty par excellence

347. I bow to the LORD
Who has EYES LIKE THE LOTUS
Taker of breath
Stealer of glances
You benumb our speech
with the extravagant beauty
of Your Eyes Divine

348. I bow to the LORD
Who is the INDWELLER IN THE LOTUS OF THE HEART
His Place of dwelling
His Seat of rest
His Throne of Glory are found
in the sacred chambers of the heart-lotus

349. I bow to the LORD
Who is the SUSTAINER OF THE BODY
Making sure that the bodies of
Your created beings function well
You suffuse them sufficiently
with Your all-strengthening Life-Breath

350. **I bow to the LORD**
Who is of GREAT GLORY
Radiant with Royal Resplendence
He shines forth His immaculate Glory
and bathes His Creation in
His Golden colored Effulgence

351. **I bow to the LORD**
Who is IMMENSELY EXPANDED
Vast is the Aura of His Being
Endless are the varieties of His Forms
Incomprehensible is His Expansion
Forever humbling is this inquiry
of the truly earnest seeker

352. **I bow to the LORD**
Who is the ANCIENT SELF
Standing unsupported
You are the Self of all selves
for all times past and
all times to come

353. **I bow to the LORD**
Who is the GREAT EYE
As the Father Supreme
His all-piercing Glance keeps check
As the Mother Divine
the all-compassionate Look
soothes all creation

354. **I bow to the LORD**
Who is the EAGLE-BANNERED
The mighty Eagle carries Him
on His Divine Flight
The soaring Wings are celebrated
as His flowing Flag

355. **I bow to the LORD**
Who is UNRIVALLED
O Lord of Glory
We have nothing with which to compare You
In helplessness we raise up our eyes
and hope that You will grant us
a glimpse of Your Vastness

356. **I bow to the LORD**
Who is SELF-LUMINOUS
The dull matter of the body
is made vibrant by
the illuminating touch of the Divine
only He Himself shines forth through all

357. **I bow to the LORD**
Who is the TERRIBLE
Unable to understand His Ways
we fear His Mightiness
and in reverence we submit
to His unquestionable Authority

358. **I bow to the LORD**
Who is the COGNIZOR OF TIME
As the Creator of Illusion
You manifest the playful thought of Time
and everything marches to its beat
in search of the Eternal One

359. **I bow to the LORD**
Who is the RECIPIENT OF OBLATIONS
Always grateful for the offerings
He imbibes the gifts of the Sacrifice
and thereby graces the giver
with His all-benevolent Smile

360. **I bow to the LORD**
Who is REALIZED THROUGH INQUIRY
Earnest seeking and
humble reverence combined with
thorough discrimination brings about
Knowledge Supreme
The Key to His Temple of Divine Light

361. **I bow to the LORD**
Who is the CONSORT OF LAKSHMI
Unable to bear separation from You
Goddess Lakshmi has secured
Her Place of Dwelling on Your Chest
Never does Her Glance stray away

362. **I bow to the LORD**
Who is EVER-VICTORIOUS
Asserting only the Good
no wrong doing can approach
Your mighty Will and
all games of the Dark have to withdraw

363. **I bow to the LORD**
Who is IMPERISHABLE
Beyond destruction He stands
Eternally free
Self-sustaining
Undiminishing in Glory

364. **I bow to the LORD**
Who is the FISH INCARNATION
Wondrous is the Form
of Your first Descent
Dazzling are the Actions
You perform in order to save Righteousness

365. **I bow to the LORD**
Who is the PATH
All seekers ultimately find Him
For He alone is the Path
He alone knows the Royal Road
He alone is the Key to the Temple Divine

366. **I bow to the LORD**
Who is the CAUSE
The primeval Thought of Creation
stems from His Mind
The primary Cause of all things
past, present and future

367. **I bow to the LORD**
Who is DAMODARA
His Mind is the brilliant Jewel
Perpetually polished
by His Storehouse of Self-control
Sending forth worlds of perfection
He is the Lord of All

368. **I bow to the LORD**
Who is ALL-ENDURING
Knowing the Secret of Time
He comprehends Its Waves
and endures patiently
Its phantom Plays

369. **I bow to the LORD**
Who is the BEARER OF THE EARTH
O Glorious Nature
Majestic Mountains
Stately Forests
You are the visible Whispers of His Voice

370. I bow to the LORD
Who is the EVER-FORTUNATE
Endowing Himself with a mortal frame
He is endlessly surrounded
with all that is benevolent
all that is prosperous
for He is all Glory

371. I bow to the LORD
Who is the SWIFTEST
Knowing all cause
His Travel to the multitudes of effects
knows no Time
Distance is unknown to Him

372. I bow to the LORD
Who is the GREAT CONSUMER
Claiming all that is His
He folds unto Himself
all that was extended
from His sparkling Fire

373. I bow to the LORD
Who is the ORIGINATOR
Thinking His Thoughts
is what brought about Creation
The intricate Play of Light
projected upon the screen
of the stillest simplicity

374. I bow to the LORD
Who is the AGITATOR
Stirring up the Silence Absolute
He brought forth the Unmanifested
into the multitudes of the Manifested
He is the Supreme Instigator

375. I bow to the LORD
Who is ILLUMINATING CONSCIOUSNESS
Praises to the One
Who is Existence
Who is Illuminating Truth
The One Who is Bliss Divine
Our Lord of Excellence

376. I bow to the LORD
Who is REPOSITORIES OF GLORIES
Containing all worlds
within His Glorious Self
He is the Storehouse of Beauty
Wealth and Wisdom Divine

377. I bow to the LORD
Who is the SUPREME LORD
Above all
Beyond everything
Within and without
is the all-pervading Lord

378. I bow to the LORD
Who is the INSTRUMENTAL CAUSE
No one but You
causes the wind to stir
It is only You
who creates motion

379. I bow to the LORD
Who is the MATERIAL CAUSE
Your Breath Divine demands
the manifestations of the worlds
Concreted matter flows forth
from the formidable Power of Your Will

380. I bow to the LORD
Who is the DOER
As the Controller of action
He propels all doings
As master of motion
He directs all plays

381. I bow to the LORD
Who is the CREATOR OF THE COSMOS
From His contemplative Stillness
arose His Word
and with immeasurable magnitude
burst forth the multitudes of
names and forms

382. I bow to the LORD
Who is INSCRUTABLE
No matter how many inquiries
or how many intellectual probings
Always beyond the human reach
is the concept of our Lord Divine
He is the Master of Mystery

383. I bow to the LORD
Who is CONCEALED
Forever hidden from the mortal eye
He remains inconceivable
He allows the veil of ignorance
to blind the people of the world

384. I bow to the LORD
Who is RESOLUTE
Being the Embodiment of the Absolute
His whole Nature is Knowledge
Annihilating all that is not
Fully embracing all that IS

385. I bow to the LORD
Who is the BASIS
All rests upon His Plan
Everything finds order in His Design
In peace His Creation unfolds
He is the Foundation of all this

386. I bow to the LORD
Who is the ABSORBER
As He pleases He withdraws
all that He has sent forth
Bringing Home the children at play
to bathe them in His Love, so glorious

387. I bow to the LORD
Who is the CONFERER OF ABODE
According to the work of each
He appoints justly
the deserved dwelling place
for those who seek to act
And all takes place within His Law of Karma

388. I bow to the LORD
Who is STEADFAST
Unbending of Purpose
His Will is permanent in steadiness
Monumental in Power
Exhibiting unequalled Equanimity

389. I bow to the LORD
Who is MOST GLORIOUS
Embellished by exquisite qualities
He is found to be
the Most Exalted One
Exceeding in Glory all that shines
More brilliant than billions of suns

390. I bow to the LORD
Who is ABSOLUTELY VIVID
Harboring Life Essential
He embodies Glory Supreme
Severely independent
His Knowledge knows no boundaries

391. I bow to the LORD
Who is EVER-CONTENTED
Abiding in boundless Eternity
endowed with perfect fearlessness
He remains utterly content
He is Bliss Incarnate

392. I bow to the LORD
Who is EVER FULL
Leaving no emptiness to be filled
No voids to be replenished
His Being saturates every space
and lacks nothing

393. I bow to the LORD
Who has the AUSPICIOUS GLANCE
Tearing apart ignorant views
Annihilating illusive fears
Evaporating all doubts
His Glance is most powerful

394. I bow to the LORD
Who is ETERNAL BLISS
In deep delight do the yogis gather
at His Lotus Feet
The Supreme Fountain from which
flows freely the blissful Nectar Divine

395. I bow to the LORD
Who is the HIGHEST REPOSE
No rest can be found
until our beings are united
into the Divine Lord of all Lords
Our Sanctuary of Repose

396. I bow to the LORD
Who is PASSIONLESS
No desires well up in Him
No wishes occur to Him
Perfectly free
He contains all fulfillment

397. I bow to the LORD
Who is the PATH
Revealing the Way to Liberation
He is the Sole Substance
of the Path to Immortality
The Royal Road to the Light Divine

398. I bow to the LORD
Who is the GUIDE
Our gracious Lord becomes the guide
when He deems the time right
for conscious reabsorbence into His Light
He is the Guide and the Path
The Beginning, the Way and the End

399. I bow to the LORD
Who is the LEADER
Always holding out the promise
of spiritual enlightenment
He is the Leader for all
No disappointment will overcome those
who follow Him

400. I bow to the LORD
Who is ACEPHALOUS
Being the Ultimate Goal
No one leads Him
No one supersedes Him
since all have to follow Him

401. I bow to the LORD
Who is the VALIANT
Bravery is synonymous with His Glory
for nothing stands in the way
of the Power of His Might
Courage excels in His Shadow

402. I bow to the LORD
Who is the BEST AMONG THE MIGHTY
O Glorious One
We are mesmerized by Your Strength
Incomparable, unfathomable
Incomprehensible is the Vastness of Your Might

403. I bow to the LORD
Who is DHARMA
His Law holds in check all beings
His Law demands obedience
His Law is righteousness
Righteousness is His Truth
Truth is His Nature

404. I bow to the LORD
Who is the HIGHEST KNOWER OF DHARMA
The Law of Righteousness
dwells within His Knowledge
He is the Commander of this Law
and Its Supreme Executive

405. I bow to the LORD
Who is the AMALGAMATOR OF ELEMENTS
He weaves together
the different elements
and produces the illusion
of the Play of Creation

406. I bow to the LORD
Who is the PURIFIER
Possessor of infinite Power
He burns up all sins
and makes Light
where there seems to be darkness

407. I bow to the LORD
Who is the LIFE-BREATH
Flow Divine of Sacred Air
He blows into the inanimate
His Breath suffuses all creation
and Life Eternal sustains all forms

408. I bow to the LORD
Who is the CREATOR AND DESTROYER OF LIFE
At the end of Times
He withdraws His Breath
and forms become formless
until once again He exhales
and Creation is created

409. I bow to the LORD
Who is OM
The first Sound is He
Its reverberations brought forth the Universe
and all thoughts and actions
rest in Its Sacred Echo

410. I bow to the LORD
Who is KING PRTHU (THE EXPANDED)
Extending to the fullest
His Expansion knows no limits
Without boundaries is His Will
He is called the Expanded One

411. I bow to the LORD
Who is the CREATOR
Manifested as Brahma
You are the Creator of the Universe
Your Thought became Word
Your Word became Form

412. I bow to the LORD
Who is the DESTROYER OF ENEMIES
Annihilator of Evil
Dispeller of Darkness
Instiller of Victories
His Truth prevails unfailingly

413. I bow to the LORD
Who is ALL-PERVADING
As the One, Who is responsible
for all Creation
He dwells in all manifestations
and spreads His unending Glory

414. I bow to the LORD
Who is the LIFE-GIVING POWER OF AIR
He is the Air of the Earth
The purifying Wave
This Sacred Element
pervading all

415. **I bow to the LORD**
Who is UNDECLINABLE VITALITY
Unexposed to change
He remains for all times
the undiminishing Source for all Strength
Expressing glorious Infinity
Emanating indelible Prowess

416. **I bow to the LORD**
Who is the LORD OF SEASONS
With the rhythm of Time
He indicates the Seasons
and presents the appointed moments
for growth and decline

417. **I bow to the LORD**
Who is AUSPICIOUS TO MEET
The Vision of the Lord
bestows the highest good
upon those most fortunate ones
whose eyes behold His Form

418. **I bow to the LORD**
Who is TIME
He invokes limitations
upon the changing worlds
and thereby weaves His Web of Time
and bewilders the mind of men

419. **I bow to the LORD**
Who is CENTERED IN INFINITE GLORY
Immovable is He
Anchored in Greatness
Perpetual in Glory
Unequalled in Auspiciousness

420. **I bow to the LORD**
Who is the RECEIVER
Supremely grateful
He gathers the offerings
of His loved Ones
and cherishes with great love
their devoted mindfulness

421. **I bow to the LORD**
Who is the TERRIBLE
As the Dictator of the Universe
He commands His demands
and in fearful fright for the Great One
all heavenly bodies
meticulously follow their course

422. **I bow to the LORD**
Who is the YEAR
Denoted as the Year
He consists of all fragments of Time
and embraces those
who are subjected to its frame

423. **I bow to the LORD**
Who is the SMART (AGILE)
Gracefully agile
He completes His Will
in great swiftness
and with keen accuracy

424. **I bow to the LORD**
Who is the RETREAT
He drapes the cloak of soft solace
around our worn shoulders
and with heavy weariness
we succumb to surrender

425. **I bow to the LORD**
Who is the MOST EFFICIENT
Precise in His Actions
Concise in Timing
He is Master of Efficiency
and reigns over the worlds in perfection

426. **I bow to the LORD**
Who is of INFINITE EXPANSION
Without horizon is His Nature
His Being reaches bottomless depth
Ceaseless is His Wave of Love
Limitless the Abundance of His Glory

427. **I bow to the LORD**
Who is FIRM AND MOTIONLESS
In stillness He contains
the Universe and its worlds
Firmly established in His Being
all rests and all is well

428. **I bow to the LORD**
Who is the MEANS OF KNOWLEDGE
A glance into His Nature
by His gracious Will
confers on our blessed souls
the Light of Knowledge Divine

429. **I bow to the LORD**
Who is IMMUTABLE SEED
Being the Ultimate Cause
for all manifestations
yet - He remains aloof
of time and change

430. I bow to the LORD
Who is the SUPPLICATED
Approached in great humbleness
by the truly earnest ones
they fervently pray
to receive His Shower of Grace

431. I bow to the LORD
Who is ALL-FULL
No roads He travels
No goals He seeks
Fully accomplished
He rests in His Fullness
Ever content

432. I bow to the LORD
Who is GREAT-SHEATHED
The five Great Layers
of this sublime Universe
are the protective covers
for His Creation of Mankind
It is His Cloak of Love

433. I bow to the LORD
Who is SUPREMELY RELISHABLE
Bliss alone is His Food
Bliss is His only Joy
No cravings He knows
for He rests eternally in Bliss Divine

434. I bow to the LORD
Who is SUPREMELY WEALTHY
Untold riches are HIs
to be enjoyed
Out of His Glorious Majesty
He creates an abundance of wealth

435. I bow to the LORD
Who is UNDEJECTED
Unswayed in Contentment
He bathes in Certainty
No sadness befalls Him
No discouragement comes near

436. I bow to the LORD
Who is SUPREMELY GROSS
Larger than large
stretches the extension
of His Cosmic Body
enfolding all measurements

437. I bow to the LORD
Who is UNBORN
Unfailing Existence
Perpetual Being
Flawless in steadiness
No reason for Birth

438. I bow to the LORD
Who is the POST OF RIGHTEOUSNESS
The Strings of Righteousness
are fastened to Him
The Cords of Correct Conduct
are bound to His spotless Soul

439. I bow to the LORD
Who is the GREAT YAGNA
Offerings sacrificed to Him
stand ablaze in His Glory
Their rewards are immeasurable
for His Grace is infinite
Such is the Lord's Greatness

440. **I bow to the LORD**
Who is the HUB OF ASTERISM
The Heavenly Bodies bow
in great reverence before
our Lord Supreme Who is
the Center of the Stellar Worlds

441. **I bow to the LORD**
Who is the MOON
Shedding rays of coolness
over the weary minds
His Love takes the Form
of the benevolent role of the Moon

442. **I bow to the LORD**
Who is OF SUPREME FORBEARANCE
He is the One
Who knows no Time
Patience is attributed
to His attribute-less Self

443. **I bow to the LORD**
Who is the SOLE SURVIVOR
Forever turned inwards
He remains untouched
by the changes of worldly life
He is the perfect Witness
The only Survivor

444. **I bow to the LORD**
Who is the WELL-WISHER
Anxious to bestow happiness
upon His Creation
He watches with great Care
over all His loved Ones

445. I bow to the LORD
Who is SACRIFICE
The Inspirer of dedication
He Himself is verily the Sacrifice
In happy joy He distributes
the offerings to the various Gods

446. I bow to the LORD
Who is FIT TO BE INVOKED BY YAGNAS
No other deserves to be
the recipient of loving worship
and genuine offerings performed
during the Sacred Sacrifices
than our Blessed Lord

447. I bow to the LORD
Who is MOST WORSHIPABLE
As His Grace alone
liberates our imprisoned minds
we direct all our worship
to our most Benevolent Lord

448. I bow to the LORD
Who is a YAGNA INVOLVING ANIMAL SACRIFICE
The Holy Purpose of the Sacrifice
is known only to Him
He is the Sacrificial Post, the inspiration,
the process and the offerings

449. I bow to the LORD
Who is SATRAM
Every Sacrifice is His
Its method is His Intent
The place, the duration
the conclusion are the expressions
of His Will Divine

450. **I bow to the LORD**
Who is the GOAL OF SADHAKAS
One-pointed are the spiritual ones
who seek only liberation
Their focus is fastened upon
the Glorious Lord of merciful Grace

451. **I bow to the LORD**
Who is the ALL-KNOWER
His all-inclusive Vision
registers the thoughts, words and deeds
of every living creature
in His manifold Universe

452. **I bow to the LORD**
Who is the EVER-LIBERATED SELF
The Creator of limitations
He enjoys the limitless
The Creator of illusive ties
He remains ever free

453. **I bow to the LORD**
Who is OMNISCIENT
Knowledge is His Power
Undiminishing in Its Extension
Accelerating in Magnitude
Penetrating through all existence

454. **I bow to the LORD**
Who is the SUPREME KNOWLEDGE
His Knowledge is the Cause
of all that takes place
His Knowledge contains all Truth,
Beauty, Bliss, and Infinity

455. I bow to the LORD
Who is of PURE VOW
He never gives up those
who seek shelter from Him
Gently but steadily He leads
all to salvation

456. I bow to the LORD
Who is of ENCHANTING COUNTENANCE
Most pleasant is the face of our Lord
Radiant with serene joy
Exuding calm and heavenly peace
So exhilarating to behold

457. I bow to the LORD
Who is SUBTLER THAN THE SUBTLEST
Escaping the necessity of a form
He goes beyond the elements
His Subtlety flows ever so freely
through all substances gross and fine

458. I bow to the LORD
Who is of AUSPICIOUS SOUNDS
Glorious is the manifestation
of His Sound in the form
of the Sacred Vedas
The Holy Scriptures of Divine Mystery

459. I bow to the LORD
Who is the CONFERER OF BOONS
Unspeakable joy does He bring
to the virtuous souls who
strive without end to please Him
Untold happiness He bestows upon them
Gracious is our Lord of Bliss

460. I bow to the LORD
Who is the DISINTERESTED FRIEND
Not moved by desire for recognition
He does not hesitate to respond
to the cry of our helpless souls
His Friendship is unconditional

461. I bow to the LORD
Who is BEAUTY INCARNATE
Forever mesmerizing is His Beauty
Our eyes are fastened upon His Form
The mind gets whisked away
by this magnetic divine attraction

462. I bow to the LORD
Who is the CONQUEROR OF ANGER
Understanding the principle of anger
He remains aloof to its poison
Fully controlled He rules
over demons and gods alike

463. I bow to the LORD
Who is of VALIANT ARMS
The stronghold of His Mighty Arms
is beyond comprehension
Many enemies have perished
by Its crushing Power

464. I bow to the LORD
Who is the TERROR OF THE WICKED
Relentless is His Demand
for righteous conduct
Any obstacle in its course
He annihilates without hesitation

465. I bow to the LORD
Who is the MIGHTY STUPEFYING FORCE
In His Desire for a momentous Play
He throws an impenetrable veil
over the minds of His children
Utterly baffled they reach out to Him
to be saved from this illusionary ignorance

466. I bow to the LORD
Who is TOTALLY INDEPENDENT
Self-sustained in all fullness
He is the Splendid One
Whose Power is the only Power
that rules over Creation

467. I bow to the LORD
Who is ALL-PERVADING
As the Creator of all created things
His Essence sustains Life
Inherent in every form
His Name sings through all

468. I bow to the LORD
Who is MANY-SOULED
Having entered the souls
of His many creations
He rules and governs His World
embodying all aspects of His Divine Nature

469. I bow to the LORD
Who is MULTI-FUNCTIONARY
Without exertion He employs
the different functions for
the maintenance of His Worlds
and with ease exercises His Authority

470. I bow to the LORD
Who is the ABODE OF THE WORLD
He is the dwelling place for all
The birthplace and the resting place
and the place of final destination
Within Him we travel the imagined journey

471. I bow to the LORD
Who is SUPREMELY AFFECTIONATE
Lord of Compassion
Bestower of Divine Grace
None has greater Love
Sweet beyond words is
Your Shower of Nectar

472. I bow to the LORD
Who is the UNIVERSAL FATHER
Diligently He looks after
His children and showers them
with Fatherly Care
He is the Protector for all

473. I bow to the LORD
Who is JEWEL-WOMBED
Bottomless deep is His Ocean of Love
Which harbors the precious gems
of His Supreme Grace, Which
enlightens the hearts of His dear ones

474. I bow to the LORD
Who is the LORD OF WEALTH
Forever prosperous is His Wealth
Undiminishing in measure
Incomparable in abundance
Glorious in Its Manifestation

475. I bow to the LORD
Who is the PROTECTOR OF DHARMA
With a vigilant Eye
He protects the Path of Right Action
ensuring right conduct
in order to guide His virtuous ones

476. I bow to the LORD
Who is DHARMIC
The actions of His Divine Incarnations
follow strictly the Path of Right Conduct
Scrupulously He sets an excellent example
for those eager to win His Grace

477. I bow to the LORD
Who is the SUPPORTER OF DHARMA
Being the Instiller of virtuous conduct
He supports its correct course
He inspires and strengthens
the will of good men

478. I bow to the LORD
Who is the EXISTENCE
He is the indefinable Absolute
The all-pervading Truth
The Supreme and Sole Reality
Existence is His only Nature

479. I bow to the LORD
Who is NON-EXISTENCE
As the mere expression of Existence
He becomes the display of Non-Existence
in a thousand Names and Forms
exhibiting the phantom play of illusive Existence

480. **I bow to the LORD**
Who is the PERISHABLE
His Manifestations fall under the law
of Time and Space
thereby are subjected to change
The perishable aspect of the Imperishable

481. **I bow to the LORD**
Who is the IMPERISHABLE
He stands alone
among the waves of change
Steadfast and supremely royal
is our Lord of August Permanence

482. **I bow to the LORD**
Who is the NON-KNOWER
Unaware of differences
His Vision does not acknowledge
varieties and modifications
He does not know diversities

483. **I bow to the LORD**
Who is the THOUSAND-RAYED
Unable to contain His Glory
He shines forth through
the thousand rays of the Sun
Light being His Breath Divine

484. **I bow to the LORD**
Who is the ALL-SUPPORTER
Unlimited in strength
He is the Bearer of all Worlds
sustaining all by His Glory
enfolding all in His Love Supreme

485. I bow to the LORD
Who is the AUTHOR OF THE SCRIPTURES
As the only Knower
of Divine Truth
His Uttering constitutes
the contents of the Sacred Scriptures

486. I bow to the LORD
Who is the EFFULGENT CONSCIOUSNESS
Clear as crystal
Shining with brilliance
He dwells uninterruptedly
in Absolute Awareness

487. I bow to the LORD
Who is ABIDING IN SATTVA
As Indweller in Goodness
He causes It to spread unceasingly
In peaceful comfort
He rests in the Haven of His Truth

488. I bow to the LORD
Who is the LION
King of Kings
His Power is unquestionable
like the Majesty of the Lion
before Whom all fear and tremble
in their acknowledgement of Its Might

489. I bow to the LORD
Who is the GREAT LORD OF BEINGS
Manifestor of all manifestations
Healer of the afflicted
Oversoul of all souls
Source of Grandeur
He is our Lord of Supreme Grace

490. **I bow to the LORD**
Who is the PRIMAL DEITY
First and foremost is He
Who decided upon Creation
and brought forth all creatures,
beings and heavenly ones

491. **I bow to the LORD**
Who is the GREAT DEITY
Sole Possessor of Divine Knowledge
He is the Supreme Deity
unapproachable by conditioned means
His Brilliance outshines the brightest Diamond

492. **I bow to the LORD**
Who is the LORD OF GODS
His Authority dominates the Divine Office
therefore all gods obey Him
and in great reverence
they pay homage to our Glorious Lord

493. **I bow to the LORD**
Who is the PRECEPTOR OF INDRA
Lovingly He instructs
the gods of all heavens
Even the great Indra
Lord of Paradise, receives His Command

494. **I bow to the LORD**
Who is the MOST EXCELLENT
Father of all Glory
Supreme Mother of Compassion
Lord of Effulgence
All-comprehensive Embodiment of the Absolute

495. I bow to the LORD
Who is the LORD OF COWS
Tenderly tending the cattle
in the meadowlands of Brindavan
the beautiful Lord Krishna
is the Gracious Lord of Cows

496. I bow to the LORD
Who is the PROTECTOR
Moved by Supreme Compassion
He is ever protective
of His Flock of created beings
Guiding every step

497. I bow to the LORD
Who is ACCESSIBLE THROUGH KNOWLEDGE
Only the Vision of the Absolute
brings us a glimpse of
the Truth of His Divine Nature
The ultimate Knowledge seeks this Grace

498. I bow to the LORD
Who is the ANCIENT
Ageless Existence
Timeless Being
Undiminishing Splendor
through all times and
for all ages to come

499. I bow to the LORD
Who is the NOURISHER OF THE ELEMENTS IN THE BODY
Ruler of the Five Elements
He sustains their course
and guides their existence
securing the perfect balance
for the human body

500. I bow to the LORD
Who is the ENJOYER
Immersed in serene bliss
He is the Supreme Enjoyer
since He alone knows His Nature
and dwells uninterruptedly in
the Glorious Essence of Divinity

501. I bow to the LORD
Who is LORD RAMA
As the Divine Incarnation
of the Glorious Rama
He assumes the playful role
of Master of the Monkeys
Hanuman being His beloved devotee

502. I bow to the LORD
Who is the BESTOWER OF MAGNIFICENT GIFTS
The Sole Receiver
of the multitudes of sacred offerings
He becomes the gracious Bestower
of the longed-for boons

503. I bow to the LORD
Who is the PARTAKER OF SOMA JUICE
Accepting the pure intention
of the sacrificial performance
He drinks with great delight
the offered Soma juice

504. I bow to the LORD
Who is the ENJOYER OF AMBROSIA
Steeped in His Divine Glory
He partakes unceasingly from
His own Fountain of Immortal Bliss
The Infinite Stream of Golden Nectar

505. **I bow to the LORD**
Who is the MOON
With sweet Care
He sends His cooling Rays by night
to nourish and sustain
all species of Life

506. **I bow to the LORD**
Who is the CONQUEROR OF ENEMIES
He enlightens the minds
even of the dull-witted ones
He softens the hearts
of the hardened skeptics

507. **I bow to the LORD**
Who is the GREATEST
Grandeur in His Cosmic Form
He alone is entitled
to be named the Greatest
Ever exceeding that which
is perceptible to the human mind

508. **I bow to the LORD**
Who is the PERFECT LEADER
Adamant about raising our consciousness
He deals heavy blows in order
to bring severe warnings to
our struggling souls drenched in dullness

509. **I bow to the LORD**
Who is the VICTORIOUS
His Deeds are very triumphant
His Guidance ensures unfailing success
His Smile bestows untold peace
He is the Perfect One

510. I bow to the LORD
Who is OF TRUTHFUL RESOLVE
Unobstructed is the fulfillment
of His Great Will
Without obstacles does His Plan
come to fruition

511. I bow to the LORD
Who is the RECIPIENT OF OFFERINGS
None other than He
is worthy of worship
and entitled to receive
the pure intentions of
those who undertake the Holy Sacrifices

512. I bow to the LORD
Who is the LORD OF THE SATTVIC
Lord of Goodness
Dweller in Peace
Your Aura bestows Truth
and enfolds all in Your glory

513. I bow to the LORD
Who is the JEEVA
Being the Supreme Self
You delight in dispersing Yourself
into many manifestations
shining forth through different manifestations

514. I bow to the LORD
Who is the WITNESS OF MODESTY
So very pleased
You look upon Your striving devotees
in their humble efforts
to express Your Glory
in great simplicity

515. **I bow to the LORD**
Who is the CONFERER OF LIBERATION
As the undisputed Ruler of all beings
He alone is the One
capable of granting liberation
His sweet Grace opens the Door to Freedom

516. **I bow to the LORD**
Who is of IMMEASURABLE STRIDE
Playfully His Strides become limitless
during His Vaamana Incarnation
His small dwarf-like Form grew mysteriously
to such an extent - capable of embracing
all creation, instilling wondrous awe

517. **I bow to the LORD**
Who is the OCEAN
All bodies of water
flow with great constancy
towards Mother Ocean
in their eagerness to merge

518. **I bow to the LORD**
Who is the INFINITE
Indefinable by Time
Immeasurable by Space
Limitless in Being
Boundless in Glory

519. **I bow to the LORD**
Who RESTS ON THE MILKY OCEAN
Fully satisfies He reclines
in peace upon the waters
in which all existence merges
O, Ocean of Milk
Sweet is Your Embrace

520. **I bow to the LORD**
Who is DEATH
Designer of Life and Death
He determines the moment
of departure for all beings
enforcing the illusive Play of Time

521. **I bow to the LORD**
Who is UNBORN
The Creator Himself
is not created
Bringing forth manifestations
yet Himself unmanifest

522. **I bow to the LORD**
Who is WORTHY OF THE HIGHEST VENERATION
Glory to our Lord God
the One to Whom
all praises flow
Our tears of blissful joy
merge into Your Ocean of Love

523. **I bow to the LORD**
Who is SELF-EXISTENT
His Eternal Existence
is Supreme Perfection
Which knows no beginning or end
Perpetually Himself is our Lord of Eternity

524. **I bow to the LORD**
Who is the CONQUEROR OF ENEMIES
Masterful He annihilates
the internal foes by splendid reasoning
Without hesitation He attacks forcefully
the various incarnations of evil

525. I bow to the LORD
Who is EVER-BLISSFUL
Consumed by unwavering joy
He remains emerged in Bliss
Adorned with the Smile of Contentment
He radiates a Golden Effulgence
of Divine Peace and loving Truth

526. I bow to the Lord
Who is PURE BLISS
Incarnation of Bliss
Embodiment of Serene Joy
Your Form is composed of Divine Nectar
Glorious is Your unfathomable Self

527. I bow to the LORD
Who is the BESTOWER OF BLISS
With great joy He gives
the Gifts of unspeakable sweet Joy
and overwhelms our simple souls
with the Flood of Heavenly Bliss

528. I bow to the LORD
Who is FREE FROM WORLDLY PLEASURES
No enjoyment He finds
in all that the senses present
for full is His Nature
He lacks nothing

529. I bow to the LORD
Who is SUPREME DHARMA
His Being is Truth
His Actions represent Truth
His Law enforces Truth
Living Truth is He
Our Lord of Supreme Dharma

530. I bow to the LORD
Who is of TRIPLE STRIDE
The three Worlds submit to His Will
In three Steps He covered these regions
as He was the glorious Vaamana
instructing the fortunate King Bali

531. I bow to the LORD
Who is MAHARSHI KAPILA
As the accomplished Master of the Vedas
He incarnated as the Sage Kapila
imparting that Supreme Knowledge
Which leads unobstructed to Enlightenment

532. I bow to the LORD
Who is the KNOWER OF CREATION
Creator of the Thought of Creation
The Knower of the Cause
The Distributor of the Effects
The primeval Essence of Multiplicity

533. I bow to the LORD
Who is the LORD OF THE EARTH
O Beloved King of all Worlds
You arc our Protector
Our loving Savior
Our glorious Father
Who showers us with meticulous Care

534. I bow to the LORD
Who is the VAAMANA INCARNATION
Celebrated for His three Strides
We adore the Lord as
the Divine Dwarf Vaamana
delighting all with His miraculous feat

535. I bow to the LORD
Who is the WITNESS OF THE THREE STATES
His ceaseless Awareness
penetrates all levels of existence
His changeless Being
watches the changing phases

536. I bow to the LORD
Who is the GREAT-HORNED
As the Divine Fish
He was endowed with a great Horn
to which was tied a boat
in order to save its occupants
from the Great Waters of the Deluge

537. I bow to the LORD
Who is the AUTHOR OF COSMIC DISSOLUTION
The Final Chapter of His Script
brings about the Dissolution
of all that He created
He withdraws His Breath and rests

538. I bow to the LORD
Who is the GREAT BOAR
As the Great Boar Varaha
He conveys to us the message
of the necessity to dive deep
into the dark recesses of our being
in order to annihilate the evil traits

539. I bow to the LORD
Who is the ONE TO BE REALIZED THROUGH KNOWLEDGE
The Sacred Words of Knowledge
open the eyes to Divine Understanding
He is the Speaker of the Holy Scriptures
He is the Giver of Enlightenment

540. I bow to the LORD
Who is of ENCHANTING ARMY
His Divine Attributes
surround Him in the form
of His ever-accompanying Flock
as Gods, Goddesses, Sages and Saints

541. I bow to the LORD
Who is ADORNED WITH GOLDEN ARMLET
Embellished by brilliant ornaments
Our Lord shines a thousand ways
The lucky armlets happily dangle on
His Gracious Arms
charming the three worlds

542. I bow to the LORD
Who is the SUPREME SECRET
He resides peacefully
in the innermost chambers
of the Temple of our heart
like a well-hidden secret

543. I bow to the LORD
Who is UNFATHOMABLE
None can gauge His Glory
Incomprehensible is His Nature
Incalculable His Ways
Immeasurable His Grace
His Divinity is of Mysterious Majesty

544. I bow to the LORD
Who is THE IMPENETRABLE
Inaccessible for the worldly man
Unapproachable for the mind-born ones
You remain ever out of reach
for those seeking to understand You

545. I bow to the LORD
Who is the WELL-CONCEALED
Inexpressible He hides beyond all words
Being the inner core of all things
He is covered by many layers
Concealed from the curious ones

546. I bow to the LORD
Who is the BEARER OF DISCUS AND MACE
With Fatherly protection He holds the Discus,
the manifestation of our whirling mind
and carefully He carries the Mace,
our faculty of the Intellect

547. I bow to the LORD
Who is the CREATOR
He is the One
Who keeps in order
the Laws of Time and Space
regulating His meticulous Creation

548. I bow to the LORD
Who is the AMALGAM OF CAUSES
As the Embodiment of all Cause
He embraces the various effects
Being One in all
He permeates everything

549. I bow to the LORD
Who is the INVINCIBLE
Unquestionable is the Power of His Strength
Unconquered He remains
throughout His many Incarnations
His Might is filled with Glory

550. **I bow to the LORD**
Who is KRISHNA-DVAIPAAYANA-VYAASA
Our Lord's sublime Wisdom alone
did permeate the beloved Sage Vyaasa
Uttering Your Holy Message
he spread Your Golden Radiance

551. **I bow to the LORD**
Who is the FIRM
Solid like the rock
He towers high above
the busy-ness of the worlds
Unaffected and supremely still

552. **I bow to the LORD**
Who is the ABSORBER OF THE COSMOS - YET UNCHANGEABLE
Playing all parts of His Cosmic Play
He becomes the Absorber of Your very Creation
Meanwhile He remains
the Observer of this endless process

553. **I bow to the LORD**
Who is the SETTING SUN
SpreadingHis firing Glow
He draws back the rays
at the close of the day
and bereft of daylight
the weary soul finds rest

554. **I bow to the LORD**
Who is the SON OF VARUNA
He shines forth through
the offspring of Lord Varuna
gracing the world
with His Wisdom and Love

555. I bow to the LORD
Who is the COSMIC TREE OF LIFE
Immovable in steadfastness
He spreads His Branches
with fragrant blossoms
over the restless moving world
Ceaselessly caring and protecting

556. I bow to the LORD
Who is PERVADING UNIVERSAL SPACE
He is the One
Who brings Expansion
into the hearts of those
who lovingly meditate upon Him

557. I bow to the LORD
Who is the GREAT-MINDED
His Mind beholds all forms
It sends forth Creation
lovingly protects it
and He withdraws it unto Himsself

558. I bow to the LORD
Who is BHAGAVAN
Possessor of Greatness and Beauty
Knower of Knowledge Absolute
Lord of Dispassion
Beloved of all saints and sages
He is Bhagavan

559. I bow to the LORD
Who is the DESTROYER DURING DELUGE
At times of Universal Rest
He destroys His Land of Images
and calls back all modifications
for a time of rejuvenation

560. I bow to the LORD
Who is ABSOLUTE BLISS
Reveling in Supreme Contentment
His Nature is made up
solely by Bliss Divine
Impeccable in Glory

561. I bow to the LORD
Who is ADORNED WITH THE GARLAND OF VIJAYANTEE
Embellished by a string of flowers
He spreads His Glory
far and wide beyond all horizons
O Beauteous Lord of the Five Elements

562. I bow to the LORD
Who is the WIELDER OF THE PLOUGH AS WEAPON
As Balarama He carried
along with Him the Plough
His Weapon to destroy Evil
His Instrument to protect Good

563. I bow to the LORD
Who is the SON OF ADITI
The Divine Incarnation of Vaamana,
so mysterious in Glory,
was brought forth
through the fortunate Aditi

564. I bow to the LORD
Who is RESPLENDENCE IN THE SUN
The Sun derives Its Brilliance
from our blessed Lord
Who resides in the very nucleus
of this most splendid of all heavenly bodies

565. I bow to the LORD
Who is the ENDURER
Oblivious to extremes
He passes calmly through
the pairs of opposites
Always equal-minded

566. I bow to the LORD
Who is the MOST EXALTED GOAL
No greater Home-coming
can await us
than our final return
into the Heart of our exalted Lord

567. I bow to the LORD
Who is the BEARER OF THE GLORIOUS BOW - SAARNGA
With ease and authority
He carries the Bow,
the Symbol of the sense-organs,
emphasizing His Control and
exemplifying the method of use

568. I bow to the LORD
Who is PARASURAMA - WIELDER OF THE INVINCIBLE AXE
Unconquerable prowess
was Your Attribute during
Your Incarnation as Parasurama
Doomed for defeat were Your enemies

569. I bow to the LORD
Who is MERCILESS TO THE UNRIGHTEOUS
No patience He shows
for those who tread the Dark Path
Eager to set them straight
His Punishment is severe

570. I bow to the LORD
Who is the BESTOWER OF WEALTH
He answers the prayers
of those kind-hearted souls
who seek their worldly comfort
in prosperity and abundance

571. I bow to the LORD
Who is SKY-SPANNING
Unlimited Space
is His Playground
Unceasing Expansion
is His Movement

572. I bow to the LORD
Who is the OMNISCIENT - VYASA
The Glorious Sage Vyasa,
the Compiler of the Sacred Puranas,
the Lord's all-knowing Instrument
suffused he was with the Breath of the Lord

573. I bow to the LORD
Who is the UNBORN LORD OF KNOWLEDGE
Creator of Beginning and End
He knows neither Birth or Death
For He alone is the Cause of all effects
Our Supreme Lord of Knowledge Divine

574. I bow to the LORD
Who is GLORIFIED BY THE THREE SAAMAS
Endless Praises
Songs of Glory
Ceaseless Worship
Such is the content of the Holy Saamas

575. I bow to the LORD
Who is the SINGER OF SAAMA SONGS
Sweetly He drapes us
with the unrevealed Mystery
of the sacred chanting
of the Saama Songs
Drawing us ever nearer

576. I bow to the LORD
Who is SAAMA VEDA
So beloved of Supreme Devotion
The Lord created this Glorious Veda
which enables us to reach great exhilaration
and instills unconditional Love

577. I bow to the LORD
Who is of THE NATURE OF EMANCIPATION
All bondage ceases
Every fear evaporates
Grief dissolves
in the company of the Lord

578. I bow to the LORD
Who is the REMEDY
HIsPresence alone
shall set us free
from the cycle of birth and death
inebriating us with
His healing Nectar Divine

579. I bow to the LORD
Who is the DIVINE PHYSICIAN
He hands out His Medicine
in the Form of Supreme Knowledge
through the Sacred Scriptures
It is there for all to take

580. I bow to the LORD
Who is the INSTITUTOR OF SANNYASA
At the last stage of Life
Our Lord encourages the Ways of the Recluse
Retreating from the scene of the World
enabling oneself to concentrate fully
on the worship and devotion of the Divine

581. I bow to the LORD
Who is the CALM
He inspires the noble souls
to find the calm peace
like the dark blue depth
of the turbulent ocean waters

582. I bow to the LORD
Who is ALL-SERENE
Without any pull towards
the mirages of the worlds
He dwells in perfect tranquillity,
contentment and bliss

583. I bow to the LORD
Who is the ABODE OF THE UNIVERSE
During the Time of Universal Rest
He harbors all of Creation within Himself
All that was sent forth
returns to Him and rests

584. I bow to the LORD
Who is PEACE
Total absence of Untruth
Non-existence of Darkness
No perception of Dualism
Your Being is unruffled Peace

585. **I bow to the LORD**
Who is the SUPREME GOAL
Once His Abode has been reached
No descending can re-occur
We remain ablaze with His Divine Love
having entered into His Fire of Glory

586. **I bow to the LORD**
Who is the MOST ENCHANTING
His comeliness is most adoring
and with awe we fasten
our gaze upon His Divine Manifestation
Pleasing to our eyes is His Form

587. **I bow to the LORD**
Who is the CONFERER OF PEACE
Bringer of Peace
Invoker of Contentment
Delighter of our hearts
All-embracing is His Love

588. **I bow to the LORD**
Who is the CREATOR OF ALL BEINGS
Creation is His Play
This Game of Light is His Invention
bringing forth all manifestations
His Thought is all-powerful

589. **I bow to the LORD**
Who is REJOICING IN HIS CREATION
Taking much delight in His Earth
He joyfully revels in this kaleidoscope
and watches the wonders of His Creation
Supremely content is He

590. I bow to the LORD
Who is RECLINING ON SESHA - NAGA
His Bed is the Serpent
emphasizing His total Mastership
over all that the senses attract
Fully under His Control
the Serpent serves Him

591. I bow to the LORD
Who is the PROTECTOR OF THE COWS
Lifting up Govardhana Mountain
He as Lord Krishna graciously saved
His Herd of fortunate cows
and brought awe to His loved ones

592. I bow to the LORD
Who is the LORD OF THE EARTH
His Reign covers the Earth
His Love drapes its Orb
His Glory enfolds it
He is the Lord of our Glorious Earth

593. I bow to the LORD
Who is VEILED BY HIS MAYA
Creating the Veil of Ignorance
Assuming the existence of duality
The One hides behind
the scene of seeming multiplicity

594. I bow to the LORD
Who is the PERPETUAL SEER OF RIGHTEOUSNESS
His Eye beholds only the Good
His Vision is of Truth Absolute
His Actions invoke Supreme Righteousness
For He is Good, sees Good and does Good

595. I bow to the LORD
Who is the ONE WHO DELIGHTS IN DHARMA
Joyfully He witnesses
the doings of the virtuous ones
So very pleased He is
with the pure flow of goodheartedness

596. I bow to the LORD
Who is STEADFAST
Unflinching is His Decision
He fights on the battleground
till His Purpose is fulfilled
He never wavers from the Path of Truth

597. I bow to the LORD
Who is the RESTRAINED SELF
Blissfully aware of His Nature Divine
His Mind does not stray away
from the Golden Light
Which constitutes His very Being

598. I bow to the LORD
Who is the INVOLVER
With ease He folds
the macroscopic Universe
into its microscopic Form
when Time needs rest

599. I bow to the LORD
Who is the BENEFACTOR
Quickly responding to the prayers
from sincere seekers
our Lord rushes to protect
the souls in need

600. I bow to the LORD
Who is SIVA - THE AUSPICIOUS
O Sivaya
Gloriously powerful is Your Name
Supremely purifying
Mysteriously sanctifying is the Name
of our Lord of Auspiciousness

601. Who has the SREEVATSA MARK ON HIS CHEST
His Chest is adorned
with the Sreevatsa Mark
The specific indication of
the Presence of Lakshmi
The Goddess of Wealth

602. I bow to the Lord
Who is the ABODE OF SREE
Goddess Lakshmi finds
Her dwelling Place on His very Chest
Inseparable She is
from Her beloved Spouse

603. I bow to the LORD
Who is the LORD OF SREE
Cosmic Power is His Attribute
Master of Excellence
Omniscience is His Nature
Almighty is the Lord

604. I bow to the LORD
Who is the BEST AMONG THE GLORIOUS
Most knowledgeable of all knowers
Most powerful of all great Ones
Most beloved of all worshippers
Glorious is the Splendid One

605. I bow to the LORD
Who is the CONFERER OF PROSPERITY
Fond as He is of His devotees
He showers them graciously
with prosperous lives
abundant with wealth and comfort

606. I bow to the LORD
Who is the LORD OF SREE (MAHALAKSHMI)
Goddess Lakshmi choose as Her Consort
none other than the Lord Himself
Longing to be His constant Companion
She finds Her Abode on His Divine Chest

607. I bow to the LORD
Who ABIDES IN IMMACULATE HEARTS
Well-pleased with pure-heartedness
virtue and supreme devotion
He resides with sweet delight
in the temple of the hearts
of great selfless souls

608. I bow to the LORD
Who is the RECEPTACLE OF SREE
All that lends goodness
to this world of duality
flows from His ever-giving Heart
The Treasure-House of Love

609. I bow to the LORD
Who is the DISTRIBUTOR OF SREE
Fully aware of one's
merits and demerits
He bestows His Favors
upon the striving souls

610. I bow to the LORD
Who is the BEARER OF SREE
Within His ever-flowing Heart
He gently holds Sree,
the Mother of all children
the Benevolent Goddess Divine

611. I bow to the LORD
Who is the CONFERER OF SREE
The natural outpour
of His Sublime Love
rains upon those who
worship Him wholeheartedly
They become suffused with His Goodness

612. I bow to the LORD
Who is the BLISS OF FINAL EMANCIPATION
Serene joy
Calm certainty
The effulgent Absolute
This is His Nature
Which He reveals at the glorious
moment of Liberation

613. I bow to the LORD
Who is the MOST PROSPEROUS
All that is Wealth
All that is Abundance
All that is Power
finds its Essence in Him alone

614. I bow to the LORD
Who is the SHELTER OF THE THREE WORLDS
No refuge we find
other than He
No place is secure
other than His Heart

615. **I bow to the LORD**
Who has BEAUTIFUL EYES
Fathomless deep
are the Eyes Divine
Enfolding all worlds
Seeing all worlds

616. **I bow to the LORD**
Who is of BEAUTIFUL LIMBS
His Comeliness is enhanced
by the full beauty of His Limbs
Striking are His Features
capable of transporting us with sweet joy

617. **I bow to the LORD**
Who is OF IMMEASURABLE BLISS
Radiant with Joy Divine
Always full
By giving more
His Cup of Nectar keeps overflowing

618. **I bow to the LORD**
Who is OF INFINITE BLISS
His Nature sings of Glory
His Being radiates Exultation
His Contentment invokes Auspiciousness
He is the Lord of Bliss Supreme

619. **I bow to the LORD**
Who is the LORD OF LUMINARIES
Source of all Light
He lends His Brilliance
to the Heavenly Bodies
and in joy they shine

620. **I bow to the LORD**
Who is the CONQUEROR OF THE SENSES
Master of the wayward mind
He directs the senses always inwards
Perfection in tranquillity
Royal in authority

621. **I bow to the LORD**
Who is NOT SUBJECTED TO ANYONE
He escapes any imagination
Every idea falls short
Notions cannot capture Him
His Glory remains inconceivable

622. **I bow to the LORD**
Who is OF PURE FAME
Spreading gloriously
is His self-evident Truth
Pure is Its Form
Far and wide Its Effect

623. **I bow to the LORD**
Who is BEREFT OF DOUBTS
No explanations He seeks
Nowhere He searches
for His Vision is unblurred:
unobstructed clarity

624. **I bow to the LORD**
Who is the GREAT TRANSCENDENT
Beyond modification
is the Superior One
No changes to undergo
for He is the Master of Transformation

625. I bow to the LORD
Who HAS EYES EVERYWHERE
His all-pervading Awareness
harbors no dark corners
Crystal clear is His Perception
of all that is, was and will be

626. I bow to the LORD
Who is PARAMOUNT
No power can exceed His Omnipotence
No knowledge can outreach His Omniscience
No manifestation cam overshadow His Omnipresence
He is All that is

627. I bow to the LORD
Who is ETERNALLY IMMUTABLE
The One Who incurs changes
He Himself is changeless
The One Who creates the limits of Time
He Himself is timeless

628. I bow to the LORD
Who is RESTING ON EARTH
As the glorious Rama
He was reposing on the ground
during His quest to cross
the Ocean of Lanka

629. I bow to the LORD
Who is the EMBELLISHMENT OF THE WORLD
The wondrous Incarnations
of His Descents on Earth
form the most precious ornaments
the world has ever beheld

630. **I bow to the LORD**
Who is PURE EXISTENCE
Containing the Essence of All
He is the Abode of Absolute Existence
Mother Ocean enfolding
all bodies of water

631. **I bow to the LORD**
Who is BEREFT OF SORROWS
Dwelling in Contentment
He knows no grief
His Glorious Nature Divine
knows no sadness

632. **I bow to the LORD**
Who is the DESTROYER OF SORROWS
Immense is His Effulgence
even the subtle remembrance
of Him, His Name, His Glory
wipes out the sloth of Darkness

633. **I bow to the LORD**
Who is the EFFULGENT
Filling all with Light
He enables the Sun, the Moon
and other heavenly bodies
to shine forth His purifying Quality

634. **I bow to the LORD**
Who is the WORSHIPPED
Adored He is
by the greatest among the Great Ones
by the purest among the Noble Souls
by the sweet singing angels
and the law-enforcing Gods alike

635. **I bow to the LORD**
Who is the PRIMORDIAL PITCHER
Divine Container of Gold
He holds His precious Creation
within His glorious Self
He holds, He gathers, He protects

636. **I bow to the LORD**
Who is the PUREST SOUL
Uncontaminated by the waves
of the three Gunas
His Soul remains unblemished
Exquisite is His Purity

637. **I bow to the LORD**
Who is the GREAT PURIFIER
Mystical is His Majesty
the very thought of Him
profusely blesses the fortunate thinker
and at once his mind becomes purified
and his heart surges with Light

638. **I bow to the LORD**
Who is ANIRUDDHA - THE INVINCIBLE
Unconquered remains Aniruddha
Enemies flee from His Sight
His Strength is Superior
Victory befalls Him at all times

639. **I bow to the LORD**
Who is the UNVANQUISHED
No parallel match can be found
No competition exists
for the Source of His Power
is unknown to any other
than the Perfect One

640. I bow to the LORD
Who is PRADYUMNA - THE AFFLUENT
Wealth is His Attribute
for He lacks nothing
His Abundance is sacred
and forever unshakable

641. I bow to the LORD
Who is the IMMEASURABLE POWER
Stream of endless Power
Source of Strength Supreme
Inexhaustible supply of Divine Energy
These are the qualities
of our limitless Lord

642. I bow to the LORD
Who is the SLAYER OF THE ASURA KAALANEMI
The Demon of Time
stands no chance
against the Lord of Infinity
Creator and Master of Time

643. I bow to the LORD
Who is the VALIANT VICTOR
Delighting in the prevalence
of Good over Evil
He strikes with confidence
those who try to obscure
His Pathway to Light

644. I bow to the LORD
Who is SOURI (VAASUDEVA)
Fortunate are the ones
born in the line of Vasudeva
for the Most Exalted One
took form in his house as Lord Krishna

645. I bow to the LORD
Who is the LORD OF THE VALIANT
Unimaginable is His Prowess
The Gods in Heaven know of
this unfathomable Secret
and in awe they bow
before the undefeatable One

646. I bow to the LORD
Who is the SELF OF THE THREE WORLDS
Inhabitant of all places
Filler of every space
Designer of the Universe
Embodiment of all Worlds

647. I bow to the LORD
Who is the GREAT PROPRIETOR OF THE THREE WORLDS
Without Your Command nothing stirs
Without Your Approval Life-Breath halts
Your Authority reigns through all lands
Your Empire enfolds all regions

648. I bow to the LORD
Who is KESAVA
Shining forth His Radiance
Spreading His Light to all corners
This Brilliant Lord
is called Kesava

649. I bow to the LORD
Who is the SLAYER OF THE ASURA KESI
The demon Kesi in the form of a horse
demonstrated great strength and
forceful intent to kill Lord Krishna
But without exertion the Glorious Lord
brought an end to his evil life

650. I bow to the LORD
Who is HARI - THE DESTROYER OF THE SORROWS OF SAMSARA
Fruitless are the attempts
of the seductive Maya
once Sri Hari is pleased
His Grace liberates the fortunate soul

651. I bow to the LORD
Who is the INCARNATION OF LOVE
Embodiment of Enlightenment
Source of all solutions
Eraser of obstacles
He is the Bountiful Giver of Love

652. I bow to the LORD
Who is the FULFILLER OF DESIRES
Holding out the promise
of the fulfillment of desires
He gently calls His wayward children
and leads them back to their Homeland

653. I bow to the LORD
Who is the SATIATED
Overflowing with sweet contentment
our blissful Lord does not
know the restlessness of desire
Serene joy constitutes His very Nature

654. I bow to the LORD
Who is SUPREMELY HANDSOME
Soul-ravishing is His Beauty
His Sublime Form haunts our minds
Our hearts know no other rest
than in the sacred contemplation
of His Divine Countenance

655. I bow to the LORD
Who is the PROMULGATOR OF THE SCRIPTURES
Eager to bestow on mankind
the Light of His Wisdom
He brought forth the Sacred Scriptures
expounding His Truth Absolute

656. I bow to the LORD
Who is of INDESCRIBABLE FORM
Beyond modification is He
Our limited minds are unable
to describe the Limitless One
Utterly indefinable He remains

657. I bow to the LORD
Who is ALL-PERVADING
His August Glory
cannot be halted
In all Its Splendor
It permeates all that is

658. I bow to the LORD
Who is the COURAGEOUS
Fully endowed with power
You reign with authority
and display calmly
the virtues of Courage and Strength

659. I bow to the LORD
Who is the INFINITE
There are no boundaries
to 'everywhere'
There are no limitations
to 'everything'
The Source is our Lord
Infinite is His Supply

660. I bow to the LORD
Who is ARJUNA - CONQUEROR OF WEALTH
His Victory over the Kingdoms
in the Four Quarters
brought him abundant wealth,
a powerful name and wide-spread fame

661. I bow to the LORD
Who is PATRON OF BRAHMAN
Encouraging austerity
Invoking knowledge
Giver of the Vedas
Brahman is His Nature

662. I bow to the LORD
Who is the AUTHOR OF BRAHMAN
Himself the perfect Expression
of all that entails Brahman
He is the true Designer
of Its full meaning

663. I bow to the LORD
Who is the CREATOR
In the Form of Lord Brahma
He assumes the role of Creator
Manifesting His Desire
to witness His manifold Expressions

664. I bow to the LORD
Who is BRAHMAN - THE BIGGEST, VASTEST
Without end is His Knowledge
Ever-expanding is His Truth
He stands for Infinity
Our venerable Lord is Brahman

665. I bow to the LORD
Who is the PROMOTER OF BRAHMAN
His Call to imbibe His Truth
to partake of His Knowledge
induces strongly the desire
for the performance of austerities

666. I bow to the LORD
Who is the KNOWER OF BRAHMAN
The true purport of His Words
is known only to Him
Knower of all
He radiates His Blissful Nature
for all to receive

667. I bow to the LORD
Who is the EXPERIENCER OF THE ONE REALITY
Supreme Father of Reality
Divine Mother of Truth
The only capable Expounder
of the everlasting Absolute

668. I bow to the LORD
Who is APPURTENANT OF BRAHMAN
Inherent in Him
lies the sublime Essence
of Austerity, Divine Knowledge,
Eternal Truth and Majestic Beauty

669. I bow to the LORD
Who is the SOURCE OF BRAHMAN
His Being contains the Vedas
His every Word reveals Its Meaning
His every motion confirms Its Sacredness
O Glorious Lord of Absolute Existence

670. I bow to the LORD
Who is the BELOVED OF THE BRAHMANAS
Full of sweet Love
the Great Souls of pure intentions
worship the Lord of Excellence
with all their hearts, minds and souls

671. I bow to the LORD
Who is OF WIDE STRIDE
His Steps cover the whole of Creation
thus overseeing His Worlds
The microscopic Manifest
of the macroscopic Unmanifest

672. I bow to the LORD
Who is the PERFORMER OF GREAT DEEDS
Grandeur is His Trademark
Splendor in His Expressions
Silent Glory in His Infinite Creation
Unequalled by His Deeds

673. I bow to the LORD
Who is OF GREAT RESPLENDENCE
No light shines forth
from any other Source
than from the Brilliance
of the radiating Aura
of our immortal Lord

674. I bow to the LORD
Who is the GREAT SERPENT
Displaying His formidable Strength
through all great creatures
He exhibits His Power
through the manifestation of the Serpent Vasuki

675. **I bow to the LORD**
Who is the GREAT SACRIFICE
Among the strong He is the Mightiest
Among the Gods He is the Supreme Lord
Among the sacred Sacrifices
He is the Glorious Asvamedha

676. **I bow to the LORD**
Who is the PERFORMER OF GREAT YAGNAS
For the interest of the well-being
of His Worlds
He undertakes the Sacrifices
cleansing the Aura of His Universe

677. **I bow to the LORD**
Who is the GREAT YAGNA
More powerful than
all utterings of praise
is the silent repetition
of His Holy Mantras

678. **I bow to the LORD**
Who is the GREAT OBLATION
His own Creation - the Universe
is offered to Him
That which came from Him
once again returns to Him

679. **I bow to the LORD**
Who is the EULOGIZED
Gratefulness flows to Him
He is the One
Who is eternally praised
Songs of Glory burst forth
from the blessed souls
steeped in supreme devotion

680. **I bow to the LORD**
Who is PROPITIATED BY PRAYER
Our Gracious Lord
dwells in delight
when invoked by prayer
Our remembrance of Him
is the Food He consumes

681. **I bow to the LORD**
Who is the HYMN
Words of Sweetness
cannot flow without His Will
He brings forth
the exultation of His Praise

682. **I bow to the LORD**
Who is the EULOGY
He is the Inspiration
for the Song Divine
He is the Melody
that expresses His Glory

683. **I bow to the LORD**
Who is the ADORER
Resident in all
His Voice is heard
as the Singer of Praises
Glory He sings
to His Glorious Self

684. **I bow to the LORD**
Who is the LOVER OF BATTLES
Engaged always in the
protection of the Good
He enters with fervor
the battleground to destroy evil

685. I bow to the LORD
Who is the FULL
Himself enough
He knows only Bliss
Self-sufficient
His Effulgence remains undiminished

686. I bow to the LORD
Who is the FULFILLER
Your Golden Hands are always
handing out Eternal Gifts
Accomplishing all wishes
You are the ceaseless Caregiver

687. I bow to the LORD
Who is the AUSPICIOUS
His Glory is unfathomable,
of such penetrating depth that
the very remembrance of Him
clears all ways

688. I bow to the LORD
Who is OF HOLY FAME
Sacred is His Being
Whose Radiance bestows goodness
upon those who are eager to receive
He is the unfailing Cure
for all ills

689. I bow to the LORD
Who is the HEALTHY
Undefiled He remains
Immune to inflictions
from His created Worlds
His Well-Being is untouchable

690. I bow to the LORD
Who is FLEET AS THE MIND
Efficiently quick
with speedy ease
He reaches His Target,
nimbler than the mind

691. I bow to the LORD
Who is the FOUNDER OF VIDYAS (AUXILIARY SCIENCES)
The afterglow of the Vedas
were captured in the Vidyas
and gifted to the Asuras,
the jealous enemies of the Devas

692. I bow to the LORD
Who is OF GOLDEN ESSENCE
The Seed of His Creation
is of Pure Gold
His Offspring is Brahma
Whose Work brought forth the Universe

693. I bow to the LORD
Who is the MUNIFICENT BESTOWER OF WEALTH
Incalculable is His Wealth
He is the Joyous Giver
of lavish presents
to His own sweet children

694. I bow to the LORD
Who is the BESTOWER OF MOKSHA
He blesses the humble seekers
with the all-inclusive Gift
of the Vision of His Truth
and Victory is theirs forever

695. I bow to the LORD
Who is VAASUDEVA - LORD KRISHNA
The most enchanting Krishna
The Son of Vasudeva
The Joy of Brindavan
The Beloved of the Gopis

696. I bow to the LORD
Who is the INDWELLER
The Witness from within
The Onlooker from outside
Seeing all
Watching everything

697. I bow to the LORD
Who is the OMNIPRESENT
His Awareness fills all space
His Consciousness is alike
in the great and the small
in the rich and the poor

698. I bow to the LORD
Who is the OBLATION
Fond of the Sacredness
of Holy Sacrifices
He becomes the Offering
in order to enjoy the process of Worship

699. I bow to the LORD
Who is the GOOD OF THE GOOD
He is the Supreme Quality
of the Supreme Ones
He is the Glory
in those who spread Light

700. **I bow to the LORD**
Who is OF VIRTUOUS ACTIONS
Beneficial to all
are His Wondrous Doings
Affecting everyone
Protecting His helpless Flock

701. **I bow to the LORD**
Who is the ABSOLUTE EXISTENCE
His Realm is of Pure Stillness
His Being does not tolerate
the presence of another
All that is - is He

702. **I bow to the LORD**
Who is of ETERNAL GLORIES
Ceaseless Praises
are sung by the heavenly beings
to Him Who cannot be hymned
effectively and justly

703. **I bow to the LORD**
Who is the SUPREME GOAL OF THE GOOD
Restless we remain
until taken up into
His Abode of Divine Truth
His Land of Eternal Light

704. **I bow to the LORD**
Who is OF VALIANT ARMIES
Followers of unwavering devotion
constitutes His Glorious Army
Which marches steadily to Victory
Fully surrendered to Him
they do His Bidding without hesitation

705. I bow to the LORD

Who is the GLORY OF THE YADAVAS - LORD KRISHNA
The Magnificent One among the Yadus
The incomparable Lord Krishna
Blinding is His Radiance
Which scorches our selfishness

706. I bow to the LORD

Who is the ABODE OF THE GOOD
Knowing their ultimate Goal
to be the Lord's Realm
The seekers do not rest until
they have reached
His Abode of Perfect Peace

707. I bow to the LORD

Who is the ONE ATTENDED BY GOPAS
Grand was His Play as the Divine Cowherd
Accompanied He was by great souls
Those endowed with Supreme Devotion
were gathered around the Glorious Lord Krishna

708. I bow to the LORD

Who is the ABODE OF THE GREAT ELEMENTS
In His tight Embrace
He holds His Creation
All that is -
is folded within His Heart

709. I bow to the LORD

Who ENVELOPS THE WORLD WITH HIS MAYA
Hiding His Doership
behind the Veil of Illusion
He becomes a multitude
of actors and actresses
playing the Game of Creation

710. I bow to the LORD
Who is the ABODE OF LIFE-ENERGIES
Immanent in Him
lies all the Power,
all the Force, all the Sustenance
of Life and its Forms

711. I bow to the LORD
Who is of LIMITLESS GLORY AND POWER
His Being is Supreme
for nothing surpasses His Glory
His Power is inexhaustible
His Might consists of Eternal Golden Light

712. I bow to the LORD
Who is the DESTROYER OF PRIDE
Impatient He is
for us to love Him unconditionally
therefore He quickly pulls out
the fast-growing weeds of egotistical pride

713. I bow to the LORD
Who is the GIVER OF PRIDE
He augments the feelings
of noble Self-confidence
The Awareness of Self-worth
which leads to the glorious Selfless One

714. I bow to the LORD
Who is EFFLUENT WITH INFINITE BLISS
No lack He experiences
for shortcomings He knows not
Within Him wells up the Fountain of Bliss
surrounding Him with perpetual Joy

715. I bow to the LORD
Who is the INCOMPREHENSIBLE
His Glory too glorious to be perceived
His Majesty too majestic to be comprehended
His sweet Grace alone enables one
to taste the Nectar of His Infinite Love

716. I bow to the LORD
Who is the UNVANQUISHED
Unperturbed, unplagued
Untouched. unconquered
by the onslaught of vicious enemies
Our Regal Lord is ineffable

717. I bow to the LORD
Who is of UNIVERSAL FORM
Himself permeating
all of Creation
His Form is the Body of the Universe
He is the Microcosmos
as well as the Macrocosmos

718. I bow to the LORD
Who is of GREAT FORM DIVINE
Reclining on the Serpent-bed
rests the formidable Lord
Embellishing His Royalty in every aspect
the Serpent is worthy of holding the Great One

719. I bow to the LORD
Who is of RESPLENDENT FORM
His Knowledge spreads Divine Lustre
His Truth radiates Effulgence
His Love makes brilliant
the darkest recesses of the Universe

720. I bow to the LORD
Who is the FORMLESS
His Total Existence
is contained within Himself
The Self Which needs
no manifestation, no name, no form

721. I bow to the LORD
Who is the MULTI-FORMED
Out of Love
for the lost ones of His Creation
He takes Form
and delights them by guiding them
safely Home

722. I bow to the LORD
Who is the UNMANIFEST
Evading conclusions
He remains uncaptured
by the restless minds
No definitions can describe Him
Their limitations He exceeds

723. I bow to the LORD
Who is of MYRIAD FORMS
Seeking the correct course
for His bountiful Creation
He descends in various Forms
to different degrees for several reasons

724. I bow to the LORD
Who is of NUMEROUS COUNTENANCE
Plentiful are the faces
in this world
Numberless His Concrete Expressions
All are His
He is all

725. **I bow to the LORD**
Who is the ONE
Self-evident Truth
Self-sufficient Existence
Selfless Bliss
He is That

726. **I bow to the LORD**
Who is the MANY
Multiplicity is His Form
Manifestation is His Expression
Creation is His Will
He is the One
desirous of becoming many

727. **I bow to the LORD**
Who is SAVA-SOMA SACRIFICE
O Holy Sacrifice
during Which Soma is made
Blessed is the Grace
showered upon the participants

728. **I bow to the LORD**
Who is SUPREME HAPPINESS
Glorious Joy
Divine Contentment
Infinite Peace
Fountain of Bliss

729. **I bow to the LORD**
Who is WHAT
All inquiries lead to Him
All probing halts at His Being
His Majesty is impenetrable
His Nature inexplicable

730. I bow to the LORD
Who is WHICH (SELF-EXISTENT)
Perpetually Self-sustaining
He is Infinite Being
The indefinable Absolute
Truth, Existence, Bliss

731. I bow to the LORD
Who is THAT
Limitless Expansion
August Majesty
Ever-present Eternity
All-knowing
All-powerful

732. I bow to the LORD
Who is the SUPREME STATE
All efforts come to rest
Every struggle finds its fulfillment
in the Loving Heart
of our glorious Lord

733. I bow to the LORD
Who is the UNIVERSAL FRIEND
Knower of all subjects
Dissolver of all doubts
Healer of all wounds
All-embracing is Your Loving Presence

734. I bow to the LORD
Who is the LORD OF THE WORLD
He is the strict Commander
The meticulous Director
The compassionate Onlooker
The detached Witness

735. **I bow to the LORD**
Who is MADHAVA
Ruler of the Universe
He is the Lord of Perfection
Distributor of Glory
Incarnation of Divine Truth

736. **I bow to the LORD**
Who is AFFECTIONATE TOWARDS DEVOTEES
Extending His loving Arms
towards the Truth-seeking devotees
He embraces them
with the Glow of His Glory

737. **I bow to the LORD**
Who is GOLDEN COLORED
Infinite warm is His unique Love
Deep gold colors His Radiance
Inviting Creation to imbibe
the Nectar of Supreme Divinity

738. **I bow to the LORD**
Who has GOLDEN LIMBS
Shining brightly toward all sides
We perceive Him as Gold
Gold are His Lotus Hands
Effulgent are His Golden Feet

739. **I bow to the LORD**
Who is of ELEGANT FORM
Elegance has reached its limit
in the Sculpture of His Form
Charm has exceeded her boundaries
in the magnificent manifestation
of the Lord of all Blessings

740. I bow to the LORD
Who is ADORNED WITH LOVELY ARMLETS
His Lustre is enhanced
by the charm of bracelets
His Beauty makes shine
brightly their lovely purpose

741. I bow to the LORD
Who is the SLAYER OF VALIANT HEROES
Out of need to protect
His devoted ones
He terminated the lives
of the vicious rulers

742. I bow to the LORD
Who is the PEERLESS
Incomparable - He remains alone
Unfathomable - He enjoys solitude
Incomprehensible - He stays beyond reach
Unequalled - He knows no companions

743. I bow to the LORD
Who is THE VOID
Not recognizable by qualities
He is the Nothing Which is all
Not describable by attributes
all definitions fade into the Void

744. I bow to the LORD
Who is DEVOID OF DESIRES
Utterly content
He knows not the wanderings
of the searching mind
Full is His Divinity
Auspicious His Blessing

745. I bow to the LORD
Who is the MOTIONLESS
His Essence is immobilized
in Truth, Existence and Bliss
Motionless still is
the Majesty of His Aura Divine

746. I bow to the LORD
Who is the MOVING
Source of all movement
He initiates motion
Nothing stirs without His Will
No one breathes without His Breath

747. I bow to the LORD
Who is the MODEST
Pride does not attach
to the One Who remains
without identification
His Flow of Purity never halts

748. I bow to the LORD
Who is the BESTOWER OF HONOR
Allowing the sense of doership
in His Game of Maya
He fancies the worldly minds
with feelings of honor

749. I bow to the LORD
Who is the VENERABLE
Beloved of all devotees
Adored by His many children
Worshipped by the great Saints
Revered by His Flock
of Gods, Goddesses and celestial Beings

750. I bow to the LORD
Who is the LORD OF THE UNIVERSE
His Will is the Only Authority
Which reigns over all worlds
Indisputable is His Lordship
Grand is His Kingdom

751. I bow to the LORD
Who is the SUPPORTER OF THE THREE WORLDS
Lender of Beauty
He made charming
the Three Worlds of His Creation
His Supreme Masterwork of Art

752. I bow to the LORD
Who is PURE INTELLIGENCE
Compact Wisdom
constitutes His Nature
Instant Intelligence
is His Trademark

753. I bow to the LORD
Who is BORN FROM A SACRIFICE
Pleased with the pure intention
of the participants of the Holy Sacrifice
He makes known His Presence
to the Blessed Assembly

754. I bow to the LORD
Who is the FORTUNATE
Blissful is the Splendid One
for He remains ever full
Undesirous of anything
He is the Richest One

755. I bow to the LORD
Who is OF INFALLIBLE INTELLIGENCE
Generous with His Intelligence
the fortunate devotee receives Its Fruit
and finds his understanding
brightened with the Light
of the ever-giving Lord

756. I bow to the LORD
Who is the SUBSTRATUM OF THE EARTH
Allowing the worlds to blossom
His Glory provides the foundation
for His Field of Action
Glorious in Its Essence
and glorious in Its Manifestation

757. I bow to the LORD
Who is the SHOWERER OF RADIANCE
Distributor of Light
Giver of Joy
Unceasingly He pleases
our dry hearts with
the Golden Rain of His Nectar

758. I bow to the LORD
Who is the RADIANT
Supremely Effulgent
The Perfect One enlivens
all Four Corners
with His Lustre of Magnificence

759. I bow to the LORD
Who is the GREATEST WARRIOR
No weapon is more effective
than the Will of our Almighty Lord
Stronger than the largest army
is His purposeful Thought

760. I bow to the LORD
Who is the SOLE RECIPIENT
Filled with happiness
our Lord is utterly moved
by the sacred gifts
His pure-hearted devotees offer Him

761. I bow to the LORD
Who is the ABSORBER
Keeping everything
within boundaries
He determines the Time-span
between Creation and Destruction

762. I bow to the LORD
Who is the FULFILLER OF DESIRES
Calling to their attention
the need for prayer
He quickly grants
the pleas of the crying souls

763. I bow to the LORD
Who has MANY HORNS
Within our Lord
lie the four states of consciousness
in perfect harmony
in absolute balance

764. I bow to the LORD
Who is INVOKED THROUGH MANTRAS
Repeatedly called upon
by the Sacred Melody
of Holy Mantras
our Lord of Supreme Mercy appears

765. I bow to the LORD
Who has FOUR FORMS
His Absolute Nature embraces
the four Aspects of Awareness
The state of wakefulness,
dream, deep sleep and
the Consciousness which pervades all these

766. I bow to the LORD
Who has FOUR ARMS
His Form is complete
while holding the Conch, the Mace,
the Discus and the Lotus
He enthralls His Devotees

767. I bow to the LORD
Who is of FOUR-FOLD MANIFESTATION
Personified as Vasudeva
we detect the Tranquil One
The Infinite excels in Sankarsana
Pradyumna presides over understanding
and Aniruddha controls the senses

768. I bow to the LORD
Who is the ULTIMATE GOAL OF THE FOUR
He is the One
to be reached at the end
of the four stages of life
Our final destination

769. I bow to the LORD
Who is of FOURFOLD INNER EQUIPMENT
Balanced within Him
we find the efficient faculties
of the mind and the ego,
the intellect and reason

770. **I bow to the LORD**
Who is the SOURCE OF THE FOUR ASPIRATIONS
He is the Instiller
and the Fulfiller
of the longing for righteousness,
wealth, desires and liberation

771. **I bow to the LORD**
Who is the KNOWER OF THE FOUR VEDAS
Only He knows
the full depth of His Sacred Scriptures
His Spoken Word
carries the Glory of His Mystery

772. **I bow to the LORD**
Who is the NUCLEUS OF THE UNIVERSE
Center of all Life
He penetrates through all spheres
Every part of Him
enfolds the Whole of Creation

773. **I bow to the LORD**
Who is the EFFICIENT WHEEL OF LIFE
He starts the whirling
of the illusive Time
creating a mirage of images
confounding the minds of men

774. **I bow to the LORD**
Who is the UNCONCERNED
Knowing the all-pervading Truth
He is not captivated
by the alluring appearances
of the World of the Senses

775. **I bow to the LORD**
Who is the INVINCIBLE
Infallible is His Mastership
Unconquerable His indomitable Strength
He alone is the Source
of all Might and Majesty

776. **I bow to the LORD**
Who is the INSURMOUNTABLE
Invoked by awe
for the Lord of all Lords
the elements and heavenly bodies
diligently follow His Command

777. **I bow to the Lord**
Who is the UNATTAINABLE
Concealed from the mind
He remains out of sight
for those who try to confine Him
Attainable only by
the full blossoming of the heart

778. **I bow to the LORD**
Who is the INACCESSIBLE
Well hidden
is the secret Hiding Place
Only the Key of Purity
might open the Door to His Sanctuary

779. **I bow to the LORD**
Who is the ARDUOUS
Many disturbances
have to be met
Plenty of obstacles
need to be overcome
before we come to His Holy Presence

780. I bow to the LORD
In Whom it is DIFFICULT TO ABIDE
Only the pure of heart
are consciously aware
of the Resplendent Resident
in their hearts
Not easily captured is the Supreme One

781. I bow to the LORD
Who is the SLAYER OF ASURAS
The followers of the Dark Path
meet their end in the confrontation
with His Divine Incarnations
His Light tolerates no darkness

782. I bow to the LORD
Who is of BEWITCHING BEAUTY
Inebriating is the Nectar
of His beauteous Form
Our hearts are transformed
by the drinking of this Divine Gift

783. I bow to the LORD
Who is ACCESSIBLE THROUGH OM
The Primordial Sound
leads the willing soul
into the Realm of the Lord Supreme
Serene and of unfathomable depth
It carries our souls Home

784. I bow to the LORD
Who is the BEAUTIFULLY EXPANDED
His indefinite Power
is expressed in His infinite Strength
colored by rainbows
of endless manifestations

785. I bow to the LORD
Who is the PROGENITOR
Designer of the World Plan
He creates the set
for the various plays
and specifies their movements

786. I bow to the LORD
Who is the PERFORMER OF GLORIOUS ACTIONS
In wondrous amazement
we watch the doings of the Lord
Filled with awe
we delve in self-forgetfulness

787. I bow to the LORD
Who is the ACCOMPLISHER OF GREAT DEEDS
Intricate beyond imagination
is His Work of Art
Sublime are the results
of His Creative Will

788. I bow to the LORD
Who is OF ACCOMPLISHED DEEDS
Having asserted His Will
everything has come to fruition
the moment He created its thought
and nothing remains to be accomplished

789. I bow to the LORD
Who is the AUTHOR OF THE VEDAS
Unable to contain
His Treasure of Knowledge
He graced the worlds
with the Flow of Sacred Scriptures

790. I bow to the LORD
Who is the ULTIMATE SOURCE
His Being is the Absolute
Infinite Existence
The unending Supply
for the Worlds Manifest and Unmanifest

791. I bow to the LORD
Who is of PEERLESS BEAUTY
Captivating is His Charm
His Movements of Superb Grace
make dazzle the human mind
and we bow with great reverence
before the Beautiful One

792. I bow to the LORD
Who is the COMPASSIONATE
How gentle is His Sweetness,
so subtle - yet so overpowering
His Compassion melts our hearts
and in peaceful joy we lay ourselves
to rest at His Golden Feet

793. I bow to the LORD
Who is OF LUSTROUS NAVEL
Embellished by a beautiful navel
He makes radiant
this unique Seat of Brahma,
the Source of all Creation

794. I bow to the LORD
Who has ENCHANTING EYES
His Eyes shine forth
the Depth of the Fountain
of His Wisdom and Divine Love
and fully mesmerized
we gaze into this Wonder

795. I bow to the LORD
Who is the SUN (THE MOST WORSHIPFUL)
Who else could be worthy
of all adoration
than the One Most High
The One Supreme Essence
Glory to Him, our Beloved Lord

796. I bow to the LORD
Who is the BESTOWER OF FOOD
Provider of Sustenance
He showers His children
with nourishment and
lovingly takes care of their well-being

797. I bow to the LORD
Who is the HORNED (MATSYA INCARNATION)
Excelling in efficiency
are the Incarnations of the Divine
During the Great Dissolution
He came as the rescuer, the Horned Fish,
pulling the Earth in the form of a boat

798. I bow to the LORD
Who is the VICTORIOUS
Effortless like a cool breeze
He sweeps away the enemy
and brings to safety
His Flock of helpless ones

799. I bow to the LORD
Who is the OMNISCIENT AND VICTORIOUS
Lord of All-pervading Awareness
Knower of every detail
Unconquerable is He
Invincible and of Glorious Might

800. **I bow to the LORD**
Who has GOLDEN LIMBS
Pure in all aspects
He radiates through all limbs
Of deep gold is the color
of His blinding Effulgence

801. **I bow to the LORD**
Who is the UNRUFFLED
Desire-less
Unattached
Passion-free
Perfect calm reigns
on the Splendid Lake of His Divine Mind

802. **I bow to the LORD**
Who is the LORD OF ELOQUENCE
Emitter of the fragrance
of Absolute Knowledge
He holds in His Palm all Wisdom
He is the Founder of all Learning

803. **I bow to the LORD**
Who is the LARGE RESERVOIR OF BLISS
Of immeasurable depth
is the Lake of His Nectar
Inebriating Bliss awaits those
who delve in His Well of Truth

804. **I bow to the LORD**
Who is the GREAT CHASM
Distanced by the
all-powerful thought
Man finds himself
seemingly separate
from the Lord, our God
This distance is His Game

805. I bow to the LORD
Who is the GREAT BEING
His Being does not know 'becoming'
Unnecessary for Him is the division of Time
for Grandeur has no limitations
Faultless is His infinite Existence

806. I bow to the LORD
Who is the GREAT ABODE
He enfolds all elements
He holds all Truth
He harbors perfect Peace
He is the Storehouse of Divine Love

807. I bow to the LORD
Who is the REJOICER OF THE EARTH
Loving His Earth
He showers it with His Care
and thereby lightens its burden
and brightens it with
the Light of Joy

808. I bow to the LORD
Who is the TEARER OF THE EARTH
Violently piercing into
the very depth of the Earth
to destroy the demon Hiranyaksha
He shows us the necessity
of probing deep for removing obstacles

809. I bow to the LORD
Who is COMELY
O Beauteous Lord
Giver of Enchantment
Instiller of Rapture
Your Comeliness leaves us speechless

810. I bow to the LORD
Who is LIKE THE RAIN-BEARING CLOUD
Pregnant with the Gift of Eternal Light
He hovers over us
like the water-filled clouds
ready to shower us
with His Ocean of Love

811. I bow to the LORD
Who is the PURIFIER
Sacred is His Form
Holy is His Name
Wise is the one who remembers Him
for pure becomes his fortunate soul

812. I bow to the LORD
Who is the OMNISCIENT CONSCIOUSNESS
Sleep does not befall Him
Peacefully alert
He remains steeped
in His all-knowing Awareness

813. I bow to the LORD
Who is the DESIRER OF IMMORTALITY
His only Wish is to bestow
Eternal Life upon the enslaved soul
Holding out the Nectar of Immortal Bliss
He frees those who partake of it

814. I bow to the LORD
Who is of IMMORTAL FORM
His Form does not undergo change
His Being is equanimity personified
His Existence is eternal
Undecaying - undying
Infinite and unfathomable is He

815. I bow to the LORD
Who is OMNISCIENT
Always established in the Eternal Present
He know the secrets
of Past and Future
of Cause and Effect

816. I bow to the LORD
Who is the ONE HAVING FACES ALL AROUND
One Life-Energy
Multiple Expressions
He is the Variety
He is the Unity

817. I bow to the LORD
Who is EASILY ATTAINABLE
Absorption in loving thought
solely towards the Lord, our God
paves the way
to His all-embracing Heart
and assures Holy Salvation

818. I bow to the LORD
Who is of VIRTUOUS VOWS
Detached from His Actions
He displays perfect Purity
and enhances the nobility
of the observance of virtuous vows

819. I bow to the LORD
Who is ABSOLUTE PERFECTION
Flawless is the Manifestation
of His Divine Will
Infallible is the execution
of His Determination

820. I bow to the LORD
Who is THE TRIUMPHANT
The Light of all Life
He stands triumphant
among the failing powers
of darkness and evil

821. I bow to the LORD
Who is the SCORCHER OF ENEMIES
Intolerable is the intensity
of His Divine Light
to those who oppose Truth
and in fear they disperse

822. I bow to the LORD
Who is the IMMORTAL TREE
Like the gracious tree
towering high above all
He grants peaceful shade
to the fatigued worlds

823. I bow to the LORD
Who TRANSCENDS SPACE
Not subjected to space
His Realm extends
beyond all spheres
Forever higher
forever more unimaginable

824. I bow to the LORD
Who is the TREE OF LIFE
Upside down is His Tree of Life
His Essence being anchored
up in the Heavenly Skies
with His Branches filled
with Blossoms of Love reaching down

825. I bow to the LORD
Who is the SLAYER OF CHANOORA
Challenged by Chanoora,
the great wrestler of the wicked King Kamsa,
Lord Krishna enthusiastically took to fight
and displayed supreme prowess
by efficiently bringing him to his wondrous end

826. I bow to the LORD
Who is the THOUSAND-RAYED
In our total inadequacy
of measuring Your Brilliance
we call You the Thousand-rayed
The Illuminator of Illumination

827. I bow to the LORD
Who is the SEVEN-TONGUED
Lord of Fire Who emanates
the Flame of Seven Tongues
Igniting His Worlds with
the Spirit of Life

828. I bow to the LORD
Who is the SEVEN-FLAMED
Layered with
Seven Forms of Brilliance
the God of Fire
consumes all that glooms

829. I bow to the LORD
Who is the LORD SUN
His Vehicles number Seven
as Surya - the Sungod
the One we adore
and sing praises to

830. **I bow to the LORD**
Who is THE FORMLESS
Imperceivable is His Being
Extended through all spheres
He is unfit
for the confinement of a form,
a notion or an object

831. **I bow to the LORD**
Who is THE IMMACULATE
Wholly pure
Unlimited Beauty
Serene Grace in motion
Fathomless Depth in stillness

832. **I bow to the LORD**
Who is the INCOMPREHENSIBLE
The very Giver of Knowledge
He Himself cannot be understood
The ever-moving mind
cannot comprehend the Stillness of Its Source

833. **I bow to the LORD**
Who is the GIVER OF FEAR
He instills apprehension
in those who travel murky roads
Emotions of fear
are His Instruments to turn
us toward Him, our Father of Divine Light

834. **I bow to the LORD**
Who is the DESTROYER OF FEAR
The devoted ones
are relieved from their fears
as He sweetly assures them
His Protection along their virtuous Path

835. **I bow to the LORD**
Who is THE SUBTLEST
Undetectable are the many promptings
He scatters among the various individuals
for the welfare of their being
Supremely subtle is
His Network of Divine Guidance

836. **I bow to the LORD**
Who is the GREATEST
We cannot find one
who is superior in Grandeur
who exceeds Him in Excellence
who outranks Him in Authority
He is our Lord Divine

837. **I bow to the LORD**
Who is the DELICATE
Not encased by matter
His Spirit transcends all forms
and spreads the fragrance
of the Delicate Realm of the Immaterial

838. **I bow to the LORD**
Who is the GROSSEST
Manifested through all and everything
His Being is widely expanded
and deserves to be called
the Grossest, the Largest Being of all Worlds

839. **I bow to the LORD**
Who is the SUSTAINER OF ATTRIBUTES
Bringing about Creation
Preservation and Destruction
He is the Foundation
of these attributes

840. **I bow to the LORD**
Who is DEVOID OF ATTRIBUTES
The Supreme of Supremacy
is not endowed with attributes
Being His own Cause
He stands alone
in the Fullness of His Majesty

841. **I bow to the LORD**
Who is THE GLORIOUS
As we find the Lord
indescribable and unfathomable
we can only feel close
by calling Him the Glorious One
For Glory is incomprehensible Beauty

842. **I bow to the LORD**
Who is SUPPORTED BY NONE
The Foundation for all,
needing no foundation for Himself
He Who carries the Universe
is unsupported

843. **I bow to the LORD**
Who is SELF-SUPPORTED
His Greatness is His Support
Majesty constitutes His Essence
Glory is His Being
Perfection is His Nature

844. **I bow to the LORD**
Who is OF EFFULGENT FACE
The Radiance of the Sun
is but a speck of Light
in comparison with the effulgence
of the Lotus Face of our Divine Lord

845. I bow to the LORD
Who is the MOST ANCIENT
Untraceable is His Source
For no one came before Him
His Eternal Life passes through the ages
Undiminishing with Time
Forever new - forever ancient

846. I bow to the LORD
Who is the PROGENITOR
As He wishes - so the Game unfolds
Blossoming Creation
Unmerciful Destruction
Such is our Lord of Polarities
Our Lord of Perfect Balance

847. I bow to the LORD
Who is the BEARER OF THE UNIVERSE
He is weightless
yet He projected the notion of weight
Therefore He, seemingly, carries
the weight of the Earth

848. I bow to the LORD
Who is GLORIFIED IN THE VEDAS
The Holy Scriptures sing His Praises
and garland Him with eloquent words
They bathe His Lotus Feet
with the Nectar of their sweet Devotion

849. I bow to the LORD
Who is the GREATEST YOGI
Embodiment of Supreme Knowledge
He personifies the Path and the Goal
He is the Essence of Yoga
None is greater than He

850. **I bow to the LORD**
Who is the LORD OF YOGIS
Unwavering in His Stand for Truth
He remains fully established
in Pure Self-consciousness
and uninterrupted Bliss

851. **I bow to the LORD**
Who is the GRANTER OF DESIRES
His endless Flow of Gifts
brings to each the desired fruit
of their motivated actions
Always ready to please
Always ready to give

852. **I bow to the LORD**
Who is the SEQUESTERED HEAVEN
Haven of Joy
Mansion of Peace
His Temple of Sacred Bliss
is our Eternal Home

853. **I bow to the LORD**
Who is the CHASTISER OF WORLDLY PEOPLE
Impatient with those
who embrace the world of the senses
He bestows hardships on them
in order to awaken the longing for Light

854. **I bow to the LORD**
Who is THE ANNIHILATOR
He alone is the Destroyer
It is His Will
That brings about the end
for all that lives

855. I bow to the LORD
Who is the GOLDEN LEAF
Our Lord, the Creator of the Tree of Samsara,
has graciously adorned
her branches with golden leaves,
the Truth-imbibing passages of the Vedas

856. I bow to the LORD
Who is the COMMANDER OF THE WINDS
In order to please Him
the Winds blow
in the directions desired by Him
In obedience and fear
they follow His Command

857. I bow to the LORD
Who is the WIELDER OF THE BOW
As Lord Rama He displayed
great skills in exercising the Bow
Therefore He became known
as the Wielder of the Bow

858. I bow to the LORD
Who is the MASTER OF ARCHERY
With great ease and
immaculate perfection
Lord Rama aimed and unfailingly hit
the target with His Splendid Bow

859. I bow to the LORD
Who is the SCEPTER
Unrelenting is His Sword of Discrimination
He is the Embodiment of Truth
and His every Word emits
the Highest Power of Authority

860. I bow to the LORD
Who is the CONTROLLER
By allowing discomforts
He keeps in check those
who are uncontrolled
in their indulgence
He is the Instiller of moderation

861. I bow to the LORD
Who is the SUBDUER
Controller of extremes
He restores the balance
by enforcing discipline
He invokes Divine Harmony

862. I bow to the LORD
Who is the INVINCIBLE
Powerless become His adversaries
in the confrontation with
the Supreme Might of His Majesty
Defeat is their destiny

863. I bow to the LORD
Who is ALL-ENDURING
Withstanding all seasons
of Worldly Play
He graciously stands above its illusion
and is found to be all-enduring

864. I bow to the LORD
Who is the SUPREME COMMANDER
He assigns the roles
to those most capable
of executing the purpose
of the Play of His Manifestation

865. I bow to the LORD
Who is the LAW-GIVER
The One Who commands the rules
He Himself cannot be ruled
He is beyond the limitations of Law
Infinite is our masterful Lord

866. I bow to the LORD
Who is THE IMMORTAL
Never far away is
the Lord of all ages
Eternally existent
He is our closest Companion
Immortal in Being, immortal in Love

867. I bow to the LORD
Who is SUPREMELY COURAGEOUS
Displayer of excellent Strength
Exhibitor of unwavering Courage
Illustrious is our Lord
of heroic deeds and splendid victories

868. I bow to the LORD
Who is THE SATTVIC
Of noble Truth is His Essence
Beauteous Calm is His Radiance
Goodness and Grace flow forth
in endless streams from His Nature Divine

869. I bow to the LORD
Who is THE TRUTH
He is the Absolute,
the One Supreme Reality
Those who have the awareness of this Truth
harbor His Presence in their hearts

870. I bow to the LORD
Who is the ABODE OF TRUTH AND RIGHTEOUSNESS
There where justice is evident
and compassion reigns,
in such places the Lord resides
Joyfully He dwells in
such Havens of Peace

871. I bow to the LORD
Who is SOUGHT BY SADHAKAS
Eager to reach the Ultimate Goal
seekers of Truth search for
the Shelter of His Lotus Feet
The Doorway to His Infinite Light

872. I bow to the LORD
Who is THE LOVABLE
All-loving is He
Loved by all
Giver of Supreme Compassion
Receiver of sweet Devotion

873. I bow to the LORD
Who is WORTHY OF WORSHIP
The most valuable gifts
are fit to be offered
to the Highest of all Gods
but worthier than all gifts
is our pure unconditional Love

874. I bow to the LORD
Who is THE BENEFACTOR
Immeasurable reward
awaits those who are
one-pointed in their devotion
His Response is the abundant Shower
of loving Protection and Divine Grace

875. I bow to the LORD
Who is EXHILARATING JOY
He sublimes the happiness
in His faithful devotees
and flooded with glorious joy
they move about - unmoved by the world

876. I bow to the LORD
Who TRAVERSES THE SKY (THE SUN)
As the illuminating Inhabitant
of the heavenly skies
He travels the aerial regions
and brightens its spheres

877. I bow to the LORD
Who is SELF-EFFULGENT
The Light of Understanding
The Effulgent Clarity of Divine Awareness
The Brightness of the Fire of Love,
these form the radiance of the Self

878. I bow to the LORD
Who is OF AUSPICIOUS DESIRE
Sacred is the longing
born within the pure heart
when brought into the Presence
of His all-embracing Love
Holy is the Desire for the Divine

879. I bow to the LORD
Who is the ENJOYER OF OBLATIONS
We offer to Him
and He in us receives
We give in reverence
In Bliss He receives

880. I bow to the LORD
Who is ALL-PERVADING
Ruler of all regions
Creation of all worlds
Pervader through all
Omnipresent is He

881. I bow to the LORD
Who is the ABSORBER OF VAPORS (THE SUN)
His Love scorches our hearts
Our melted beings rise ever upwards
until His Divine Compassion absorbs us
Merciful are the Rays of His sunlit Love

882. I bow to the LORD
Who is OF VARIEGATED SPLENDOR
Sweet and gentle
His Flame can glow,
yet .. with austere intensity
His Fire is ready to burst forth

883. I bow to the LORD
Who is THE SUN
He is the Glorious One
harboring all Brilliance
In motion He sets
the Wheel of Fire

884. I bow to the LORD
Who is the CAUSE OF THE UNIVERSE
Only the Formless can cause Forms
Only Silence can create Sound
Only Stillness can generate Motion
He is the Formless, the Silence, the Stillness

885. I bow to the Lord
Whose EYES ARE THE SUN
His Universal Body claims
the Sun as His Eyes
Light Eternal shines forth
from this Source of Fire

886. I bow to the LORD
Who is ENDLESS
Witness of Creation
He outlasts its Finity
Lover of all manifestations
He endures all existence
Everlasting and Infinite is the Lord

887. I bow to the LORD
Who is the CONSUMER OF OBLATIONS
The Only Recipient
He rejoices in the gifts
offered at the Sacred Sacrifices
Bliss is His Joy
Bliss is His Grace

888. I bow to the LORD
Who is the ENJOYER
Pleased with the panorama
of the worlds
He is the Delighted Viewer
of its magnificent beauty

889. I bow to the LORD
Who is the BESTOWER OF BLISS
To pieces He tears
the wrong notions of duality
and submerges us deeply
in His Divine Ocean of Supreme Love

890. I bow to the LORD
Who is MULTI-INCARNATE
Like the Loving Mother
rushing time and time again
to her helpless child
So He descends many times

891. I bow to the LORD
Who is the FIRST-BORN
His all-conscious Mind
desired Creation and
He became Form
The Lord is the First-Born

892. I bow to the LORD
Who is the UNDEJECTED
Being All in All
He is utterly free
from the need to accomplish
Free from fear of failure
Everything He is, everything He has

893. I bow to the LORD
Who is EVER-COMPASSIONATE
Unlimited in giving
Timeless in Patience
Continuous in Caring
O, beautiful Embodiment of Grace

894. I bow to the LORD
Who is the SOLE SUBSTRATUM OF THE UNIVERSE
His Being alone is Existence
His Glory alone carries Creation
His Nature is the only Support
for all manifestations

895. **I bow to the LORD**
Who is the WONDER
His Glory hides behind
the Realm of Marvel
The Radiance of Awe
seeks Him in all humility

896. **I bow to the LORD**
Who is the ETERNAL
He hands us the tool, called Time
in order to awaken our longing
for His Timeless Being
His Land of Infinite Love

897. **I bow to the LORD**
Who is the MOST ANCIENT
His Thought alone
is responsible for Creation
He is the One,
the First and the Ancient

898. **I bow to the LORD**
Who is KAPILA MUNI
O Lord of Fires
We ascribe to You the various colors
of its Divine Flames
You emerge as light red
from the subterranean Fire, called Kapila

899. **I bow to the LORD**
Who is the EVAPORATOR
He makes disappear
all that comes into His Presence
His Supreme Love quickly unites
with all that approaches Him

900. **I bow to the LORD**
Who is the IMMUTABLE
That which changes
becomes drawn into the Unchangeable
to be held forever in stillness
to remain forever in His changeless Glory

901. **I bow to the LORD**
Who is the BESTOWER OF BLESSINGS
Indescribable are His Gifts
They reach far beyond
the horizon of our expectations
We lose ourselves in His Ocean of Bliss

902. **I bow to the LORD**
Who is the BENEFACTOR
He only gives that
which benefits the recipient
Ultimate Good
being His Supreme Goal for creation

903. **I bow to the LORD**
Who is AUSPICIOUSNESS
Perpetually enveloped
by the Aura of Divinity
He is the Most Auspicious One
So wondrous to behold

904. **I bow to the LORD**
Who is the DWELLER IN AUSPICIOUSNESS
His Dwelling Place is in Radiant Glory
His Throne is found in the Heart of Truth
His Home is the Abode of Auspiciousness
He is the Only Occupant
of such a Divine Realm

905. I bow to the LORD
Who is the DEXTEROUS DISTRIBUTOR OF AUSPICIOUSNESS
Revealer of the Divine Mystery
He embraces the fortunate soul
with the wondrous awareness
of His momentous Auspiciousness

906. I bow to the LORD
Who is NOT FIERCE
He knows no anger
He entertains no attachment
Gentle are His Ways
Flowing freely is His Sweetness

907. I bow to the LORD
Who is ADORNED WITH EARRINGS
His Beauty is enhanced
by the presence of earrings
Radiant is His Form
Brilliant His Ornaments

908. I bow to the LORD
Who is the WIELDER OF THE DISCUS
Master of the illusive Mind
He holds its Power
in the shape of the fierce Discus
in His Lotus Hand
protecting the Worlds

909. I bow to the LORD
Who is the VALOROUS
Bravery, Courage and
Zeal for Victory
these are the human characteristics
He displays during His Incarnations

910. I bow to the LORD
Who is the MIGHTY COMMANDER
His Words are His Commands
His Scriptures are the Divine Law
His Message is superior to all reasoning
Supreme is His Authority

911. I bow to the LORD
Who is the INDESCRIBABLE
A thousand Words
and numberless Names
All fail to capture
His infinite Glory
His sublime Majesty

912. I bow to the LORD
Who is INVOKED BY VEDAS
Discernable through sincere study
of the mighty Vedas
The Lord allows us
a glimpse into His immeasurable Glory

913. I bow to the LORD
Who is the COOL ARBOR
He provides soothing shelter
for the weary souls
who have endured
the scorching heat of the three Worlds

914. I bow to the LORD
Who is the CREATOR OF DARKNESS
He dims the Light of Knowledge
in the worldly men
He dims the awareness of duality
in the enlightened soul
In causing Darkness
He calls us to Light

915. I bow to the LORD
Who is the NEVER-CRUEL
Not aware of desires
He does not meet with discontent
therefore He remains without anger
He is always gentle and filled with Love Divine

916. I bow to the LORD
Who is SUPREMELY SOFT
Endearing are His Divine Forms
Awe-inspiring are His Actions
Heart-warming His Words
He softens our hardened souls

917. I bow to the LORD
Who is the ADROIT
Perfectly efficient
in all His Doings
Handsome and strong
He shines forth as the Most Skillful One

918. I bow to the LORD
Who is the BOUNTIFUL GIVER
Always with us
He protects us from all sides
He showers us with attention
He is the insistent Lover of our hearts

919. I bow to the LORD
Who is SUPREMELY PATIENT
Infinity is His Nature
Timeless is His Role as the Witness
in Which impatience finds no abode
He embraces all Times

920. I bow to the LORD

Who is OF THE GREATEST WISDOM
Lord Supreme
Knower of Truth
All-pervading He is
The One Who has Knowledge Absolute

921. I bow to the LORD

Who is THE FEARLESS
Fully Self-supported
He knows no fear
He is All
and in His All-ness He is content

922. I bow to the LORD

Whose GLORY WHEN HEARD AND SUNG
MAKES THE DEVOTEE MERITORIOUS
O Mystery of all Mysteries
How sweet is the Grace,
so pure and simple
The singing of Your Name
quickly enfolds us to Your Heart

923. I bow to the LORD

Who is THE SAVIOUR
Soft at Heart
The Lord listens eagerly
for the cries of His Children
Always ready to carry them
safely to the other shore

924. I bow to the LORD

Who is the DESTROYER OF SINS
Evil tendencies and its karma
fade away by the very sight of Him
Even the remembrance of Him
purifies our heart, mind and soul

925. I bow to the LORD
Who is SUPREMELY PURE
Unmatched is the Grace
He bestows upon the devoted ones
His immense Love makes holy
and pure those who adore Him

926. I bow to the LORD
Who is the DISPELLER OF THE HORRIBLE REAM
Intolerant toward untruth
He evaporates the Great Illusion
and lays bare the Games of Falsehood
Truth He is - Truth He proclaims
Truth He manifests

927. I bow to the LORD
Who is the CULMINATOR OF THE WHIRL OF SAMSARA
He is the End of all Plays
He is the Finish of all Games
He is the Annihilator of Time
Glorious is our Destination

928. I bow to the LORD
Who is the PROTECTOR
He subsists on Goodness alone
Its protective Radiance embraces
the three Worlds and their inhabitants
All-caring is our Divine Father

929. I bow to the LORD
Who is the RIGHTEOUS
Dwelling in the hearts
of Truth-loving souls
He inspires their good actions
Verily, He is their Goodness

930. I bow to the LORD
Who is the LIFE
One Life-Force
One Perennial Being
Pure Existence
He is the Absolute

931. I bow to the LORD
Who is ALL-PERVADING
Having no Form
He inhabits all forms
Being silent
He carries all sound

932. I bow to the LORD
Who has INFINITE FORMS
Being the Essential Form
of all forms
He is all manifestations,
infinitely multiplied by Himself

933. I bow to the LORD
Who is OF INFINITE POWERS
Endless is the Source of His Supreme Might
Countless are the ways
in which He displays His Omnipotence
Wonder-struck we remain spellbound
by this most Glorious Mystery

934. I bow to the LORD
Who is the CONQUEROR OF ANGER
His Heart, so full of Love,
allows no room
for the Gloom of Anger
All shadows of discontent
fade away in His Divine Light

935. I bow to the LORD
Who is the DISPELLER OF FEARS
His Presence heralds
the lifting of the Veil of Ignorance
Sweetly He takes us Home
leaving behind the bewilderment of the worlds

936. I bow to the LORD
Who is the PERFECT JUDGE
Knowing the intentions
of the individual 'doers'
He distributes
the rightful consequences

937. I bow to the LORD
Who is the UNFATHOMABLE
Mesmerizing is the Depth of His Mystery
Blinding is the piercing Light of His Truth
Awe-inspiring the intense Vastness of His Love
No choice we have here other than
to lose ourselves in His Wondrous Glory

938. I bow to the LORD
Who is the UNIQUE DISTRIBUTOR
Only the all-pervading One
can justly gauge
how and what each person deserves and needs
And so He gives
according to His Judgment

939. I bow to the LORD
Who is the UNIQUE COMMANDER
Leader of all Deities
He instructs and directs them
in how to carry out their assigned duties
He is the Master of men and gods alike

940. **I bow to the LORD**
Who is THE SEER
All-embracing is His Vision
From His Glance we receive
the highest reward or
the most severe punishment

941. **I bow to the LORD**
Who is THE BEGINNINGLESS
No growth - no decline
No beginning - no end
No birth - no death
Essence of all Existence
This is the Perennial One

942. **I bow to the LORD**
Who is the SUBSTRATUM OF THE EARTH
All that leans upon this Earth
derives support from Him
Who is the Holder of this Planet,
its Protector and its Creator

943. **I bow to the LORD**
Who is the SPLENDOR OF THE UNIVERSE
Generously He spreads
His undiminishing Glory
over the Creation of this Universe
He clothes It with lustrous Radiance

944. **I bow to the LORD**
Who is the MOST VALOROUS
Supreme is every way
He excels in sublimity
and holds the Scepter,
signifying His Authority
His Bravery, His unparalleled Glory

945. I bow to the LORD
Who has SPLENDID ARMLETS
Beauteous to behold
is the most exalted Form
of our Lord Divine
embellished by lovely jewelry

946. I bow to the LORD
Who is the PROGENITOR
Father of all mankind
He has no ancestry
He is the First, the Only
the Eternal One

947. I bow to the LORD
Who is the PRIME CAUSE OF ALL BEINGS
His Thought is our Birthplace
His Love is our Essence
His Consciousness is our Home
In Him we are One

948. I bow to the LORD
Who is THE TERRIBLE
He is the Instiller of Fear
when He fights Untruth
Full of zeal for Righteousness
He strikes terror in the hearts
of those who walk a wayward path

949. I bow to the LORD
Who has FORMIDABLE POWERS
His endless Might causes
enemies to tremble
Unsurpassed is the Strength
He exhibits during His many Incarnations

950. I bow to the LORD
Who is the FUNDAMENTAL SUSTAINED
In Him we find the Abode
of the essential elements
He is the Foundation for all Existence
The Sustainer of the Essence

951. I bow to the LORD
Who is the SUPREME CONTROLLER
Having no superiors
He is the Absolute Command
As the Creator of all
He is the Ultimate Controller

952. I bow to the LORD
Who is BLOOMING LIKE A BLOSSOM
His Love Divine unfolds
into the flowering Universe
emitting the wondrous Fragrance
of His Supreme Grace

953. I bow to the LORD
Who is EVER-AWAKENED
No sleep overcomes Him
No clouds gather in the deep blue
of His ever-expanded Awareness
He alone has Absolute Consciousness

954. I bow to the LORD
Who is THE ASCENDENT
The Highest of all high
All manifestations are below Him
His Thought made Its Descent
and became the worlds of many forms

955. I bow to the LORD
Who is OF VIRTUOUS CONDUCT
He loves Goodness
He expresses Its Sweetness
He instills Its Virtue
He guides Its followers

956. I bow to the LORD
Who is THE LIFE-GIVER
He revives the life-less
The inanimate becomes animate
The dull become radiant
His Breath is our precious Life

957. I bow to the LORD
Who is OM
He brings forth
the Essence of all sound
Om is His Word
Creation is the effect

958. I bow to the LORD
Who is THE SUPREME MANAGER
Superb is His organizational Skill
He oversees the multitudes of beings
and guides the purpose of each
Meticulous is His Divine Management

959. I bow to the LORD
Who is SELF-CERTIFYING
No proof is needed
for the One, Whose Being
is Truth, Existence and Bliss
He defies all explanations

960. I bow to the LORD
Who is the SUBSTRATUM OF PRANAS (VITAL AIR)
Storehouse of Life-Force
He is the Carrier of Its Breath
Holder of the Vital Airs
He is the Abode for all Life

961. I bow to the LORD
Who is THE NOURISHER OF PRANAS
His attentive Thought
serves as Food for
the Vital Airs
He enlivens the Breath of Life

962. I bow to the LORD
Who is THE PRANA OF PRANAS
Lord of the Subtlest of all subtleties
He is the Master of all Airs
The Instiller of Its Life
The Supreme Prana

963. I bow to the LORD
Who is ABSOLUTE REALITY
Pristine Consciousness
Unsullied Love
Infallible Truth
Unmodified Existence

964. I bow to the LORD
Who is THE KNOWER OF REALITY
He constitutes the Essence of Reality
His Nature is Reality
He embodies fundamental Truth
Knowing Himself - He alone knows Reality

965. I bow to the LORD
Who is THE ONE SELF
Subsisting through all
Pervading every being
Sole Awareness
He is the One
The Lord of the Self

966. I bow to the LORD
Who is BEYOND MODIFICATIONS
The Process of Change
cannot touch the Eternal One
Growth and decay
find no place in His Perennial Being

967. I bow to the LORD
Who is the COSMIC SAP OF THE THREE WORLDS
He inundates the three Worlds
with His Living Water
and thus makes rotate
the Wheel of imaginary Existence

968. I bow to the LORD
Who is THE ETERNAL REDEEMER
Embodiment of Compassion
Bestower of Grace
He eagerly rescues the drowning souls
from the turbulent waters
of the Ocean of Illusion

969. I bow to the LORD
Who is the ETERNAL FATHER
Our Creation knows but One Creator
All manifestation recognizes one Source
He alone fathers all mankind
O, Lord of the Universe

970. I bow to the LORD
Who is the GREAT-GRANDSIRE
Forefather of all fathers
Creator of Lord Brahma
The Great-Grandfather of all
He is our most ancient Ancestor

971. I bow to the LORD
Who is YAGNA (SACRIFICE)
He is the Inspirer
of the various forms of Worship
His Sparkle enlivens the devotional act
Verily, He is the Sacrifice

972. I bow to the LORD
Who is the LORD OF YAGNAS
He is Love
His Expression is the Manifest
His Action is Worship
His Treasure is Yagna, the Sacrifice

973. I bow to the LORD
Who is the PERFORMER OF SACRIFICES
In charge of the Sacrifice
He is the Supreme Director
of this worshipful act
Sacred are His Deeds

974. I bow to the LORD
Who is the LIMBS OF SACRIFICE
His Divine Manifestations as the Cosmic Boar
holds all symbols of the Holy Sacrifice
The Sacrificial Gift is His Heart
The Sacrificial Rites are His Arms
The Holy Acts are His Footsteps
As such - He is the full Expression of Yagna

975. I bow to the LORD
Who is the ACCOMPLISHER OF SACRIFICES
Pleased with the beneficial results
of such Holy Undertakings
He sees to it that
all is fulfilled and accomplished

976. I bow to the LORD
Who is the PROTECTOR OF SACRIFICES
Safeguarding that which is
most dear to Him
He diligently protects
the purpose and process of the Sacrifice

977. I bow to the LORD
Who is the CREATOR OF SACRIFICES
Seeking the perfect expression
for the Holy Intent of worshipful acts
our Supreme Lord created
the glorious Sacred Scriptures

978. I bow to the LORD
Who is the ENJOYER OF SACRIFICES
Completing the circle
of instilling heartfelt devotion
and receiving adoration
He is the Silent Witness
and the Joyful Recipient

979. I bow to the LORD
Who is the RECEPTACLE OF SACRIFICES
He is the One
Who contains within Him
the Reason, the Process and the Results
of the Holy Sacrifice

980. **I bow to the LORD**
Who is the MATERIAL OF THE SACRIFICES
Sacred are the Chants
Blessed is the Worshipful Act
Holy are the Materials
For He embodies these

981. **I bow to the LORD**
Who is the PERFORMER OF THE ULTIMATE OFFERING IN SACRIFICES
Though the Sole Performer
throughout the Yagna
His Intensity heightens
at the Highlight of this Supreme Act of Worship
He excels at the Conclusive Offering
and makes vibrant the Holy Atmosphere

982. **I bow to the LORD**
Who is the SECRET OF SACRIFICES
From His Divine Knowledge
sprouts the Glorious Yagna
He holds Its sublime Secret in His Bosom
and graces us with the Flowers of His Heart

983. **I bow to the LORD**
Who is THE FOOD
He takes care of us as Sustenance
in the form of Food
He is the Nourishment
The Giver of Life

984. **I bow to the LORD**
Who is the SWALLOWER OF FOOD
Relishing His Creation
We picture Him as
the Divine Consumer of His Food,
the Manifestation of the worlds

985. I bow to the LORD
Who is the MATERIAL CAUSE
Numberless effects
with only One Cause
The responsibility rests
in the Golden Hands of our Glorious Lord

986. I bow to the LORD
Who is the SELF-BORN
Enjoying the Thought of Creation
His Manifestation became born
His selfless Self projected
the myriads of 'selves'

987. I bow to the LORD
Who is the VARAAHA INCARNATION
Adopting the Form of the Cosmic Boar Varaaha
He instilled deep reverence
into the hearts of the fortunate ones
who witnessed this auspicious Divine Incarnation

988. I bow to the LORD
Who is the SINGER OF SAAMA SONGS
Master Composer
Chanter par excellence
He thrills the Universe
with His Songs Divine

989. I bow to the LORD
Who is the JOY OF DEVAKI
O Blessed Mother Devaki
Who gave birth to the Glorious Krishna
Unparalleled joy did He bestow upon her
by choosing her as His earthly Mother

990. I bow to the LORD
Who is the CREATOR
The Manifest indicates
the all-pervading Unmanifest
Creation leads us to
the all-powerful Creator
He is the Unmanifest
He is the Supreme Creator

991. I bow to the LORD
Who is the LORD OF THE EARTH
Designer of the World
He is the Master of Its Play
He reigns with majestic Authority
over His Land of Illusion

992. I bow to the LORD
Who is the ANNIHILATOR OF SINS
Glorious is His Grace
Inconceivable Its unfathomable Depth
Our all-embracing Lord
wipes clean the murky slates
of those who remember Him fondly

993. I bow to the LORD
Who is the BEARER OF THE CONCH
PAANCHAJANYA
With sweet concern
He calls His helpless ones
to surrender the ego
and listen with rapture
to His Song Divine

994. I bow to the LORD
Who is the WIELDER OF THE NANDAKA SWORD
With impatience
He awaits His loved ones
and in His eagerness
He wields the Sword,
destroys ignorance
and brings spiritual enlightenment

995. I bow to the LORD
Who is the BEARER OF SUDARSANA CHAKRA
This Weapon instills Time
The fearless Annihilator
of all that holds sway
over the deluded mind
Merciless and fierce is
this Instrument of our Glorious Lord

996. I bow to the LORD
Who is the WIELDER OF SAARGNA BOW
Supreme Holder of the Mighty Bow
In full control He is
of the five Sense-organs
Royally He carries this Symbol
keeping within boundaries
the wayward tendencies

997. I bow to the LORD
Who is the BEARER OF THE DIVINE MACE
KAUMODAKEE
He lovingly diverts our attention
from the panoramic World
to His Ocean of Love
by using His Divine Mace,
bringing upon us discontent
with the fleeting moments of Life
His Mace sharpens our Intellects

998. I bow to the LORD
Who HOLDS THE WHEEL
Unaware of Time
He endlessly turns the Wheel
and the Dance of Illusion,
the Mirage of Existence,
the Stage for Ignorance
goes around and around
He is the Holder of the Wheel

999. I bow to the LORD
Who is the IMPERTURBARBLE
The Supreme Carrier
of the Divine Weapons
He is the Serene One
in full control
Undisturbed and brilliant in His Glory

1000. I bow to the LORD
Who is the SUPREME CONQUEROR
He is the One
Whose Will knows no obstructions
Everything turns into His Instrument
and yields to His desired Purpose
He is the Almighty Lord
The Sublime Master of all Creation
The Most Glorious One

~~~~~~~~~~
~~~~~~~~~~

SALUTATIONS TO THE GLORIOUS ONE

Who is in front of us

behind us

beside us

within us

May our thoughts be as fragrant flowers
offered at His Lotus Feet

May our every word carry the tune
of His Truth and Glory

May our actions speak silently
of His immediate Presence

IN HUMBLE REVERENCE I BOW

TO

LORD VI SHNU

WORDS OF THE WISE

The following was said about the effectiveness of the repetition of the THOUSAND NAMES OF LORD VISHNU by Bhisma, who recited these Divine Names to King Yudhisthira:

........."Hereby are described the THOUSAND DIVINE NAMES of the great Kesava.

One who daily repeats these NAMES shall never meet with anything inauspicious in this world or the next.
The devotee, who waking up early in the morning, repeats this Hymn addressed to Vasudeva, obtains fame, prominent status in society, steady wealth, supreme good, will enjoy courage and strength, will be healthy, radiant and virtuous.

> The one, who every day chants with devotion these Divine NAMES, is instantly freed from all obstacles. Free from all sins he attains to the eternal Brahman, he is always free from fear of birth, death, old age and disease. He is promised the bliss of the Self, patience, prosperity, fortitude, memory and fame.
> Lord MahaVishnu is the One, the all-comprehensible Being, Who appears as the many, He is the Essence of all beings, the Consumer of the worlds.
> Pervading the three worlds He enjoys all entities.
> Whoever desires happiness and the highest bliss should repeat this Sacred Hymn praising Lord Vishnu, composed by the sage Vyasa.
> Those who worship the Lotus-eyed One, from Whom all worlds originate and into Whom all dissolve, will never meet with defeat" ....

O fortunate reader,
Pay heed to these sacred ancient words of wisdom spoken by the Great Ones.
Imbibe deeply the holiness of their message.
Do not file me away on your bookshelf, but always keep me close.
I pray that through the reading of these THOUSAND SONGS OF LORD VISHNU ...

... may our gracious Lord has drenched your heart with His Divine Nectar

... and that He has moistened your thought-worn mind with the Flow of Blissful Tears

... that He has captivated your soul with His Golden Glory

... and that your whole being has become submerged in the Mystery of His Majesty

... for this is His Wondrous Purpose

~~~~~~~~~~
~~~~~~~~~~

Bibliography

Vishnu Sahasranama ....by Ajit B. Kapadia

Sri Vishnu Sahasranama ......commentary by Sri Sankaracharya translated into English by Swami Tapasyananda

OUR PUBLICATIONS

01.	70 QS & AS. ON PRACTICAL SPIRITUALITY AND SATHYA SAI BABA	- O.P.Vidyakar	Rs. 90
02.	A JOURNEY TO LOVE (Fourth Edition)	- David Bailey	Rs.180
03.	A JOURNEY TO LOVE (Spanish)	- David Bailey	Rs.375
04.	"ALEX" THE DOLPHIN	- Johnima Wintergate	Rs. 90
05.	A STORY OF INDIA AND PATAL BHUVANESWAR	- Jennifer Warren	Rs. 60
06.	A COMPENDIUM OF THE TEACHINGS OF SATHYA SAI BABA (Second Edition)	- Charlene Leslie-Chadan	Rs.555
07.	ASHES,ASHES WE ALL FALL DOWN	- Gloria St. John	Rs. 80
08.	BAPU TO BABA	- V.K. Narasimhan	Rs.120
09.	BHAGAVAN SRI SATHYA SAI BABA DISCOURSES IN KODAIKANAL, APRIL 96	- Pooja Kapahi	Rs.120
10.	BUDO-KA-TRUE SPIRITUAL WARRIORS	- Deena Naidu	Rs.200
11.	CRICKET FOR LOVE A Souvenir on Sri Sathya Sai Unity Cup		Rs.250
12.	CUTTING THE TIES	- Phyllis Krystal	Rs.110
13.	CUTTING MORE TIES THAT BIND	- Phyllis Krystal	Rs.120
14.	CUTTING THE TIES - WORK BOOK	- Phyllis Krystal	Rs.140
15.	DA PUTTAPARTHI A PATAL BHUVANESHWAR (Italian)	- Sandra Percy	Rs.150
16.	DEATHING (Indian Edition)	- Anya Foos-Graber	Rs.195
17.	DISCOVERING MARTIAL ARTS	- Deena Naidu	Rs.265
18.	DIVINE LEELAS OF BHAGAVAN SRI SATHYA SAI BABA	- Nagamani Purnaiya	Rs. 90
19.	EDUCATION IN HUMAN VALUES (3 Vols.) (Indian Edition)	- June Auton	Rs.750
20.	GLIMPSES OF THE DIVINE	- Birgitte Rodriguez	Rs.150
21.	GOOD CHANCES (Second Edition)	- Howard Levin	Rs.120
22.	GOD AND HIS GOSPEL	- Dr. M.N.Rao	Rs.120
23.	GOD DESCENDS ON EARTH	- Sanjay Kant	Rs. 60
24.	GOD LIVES IN INDIA	- R. K. Karanjia	Rs. 75
25.	HEART TO HEART (Reprint)	- Howard Levin	Rs.120
26.	IN QUEST OF GOD	- P.P. Arya	Rs.120
27.	KNOW THYSELF (Second Edition)	- Gerard T. Satvic	Rs.180
28.	LET ME SOW LOVE	- Doris May Gibson	Rs.120
29.	LETTERS FROM A GRANDFATHER	- S. K. Bose	Rs.180
30.	MESSAGES (JAPANEESE)	- Dr. M.N. Rao	Rs.150
31.	MIRACLES ARE MY VISITING CARDS (Indian Edition)	- Erlendur Haraldsson	Rs. 180
32.	MOHANA BALA SAI (Children's Book)	- Sai Mira	Rs.120
33.	MUKTI THE LION FINDS HIMSELF	- Gina Suritsch	Rs. 85
34.	MESSAGES FROM MY DEAREST FRIEND SAI BABA	- Elvie Bailey	Rs.130
35.	NARA NARAYANA GUFA ASHRAM Part III	- Swami Maheswaranand	Rs. 20
36.	PRASANTHI GUIDE	- R. Padmanaban	Rs. 50
37.	SAI BABA GITA	- Al Drucker	Rs.240
38.	SAI BABA: THE ETERNAL COMPANION	- B. P. Misra	Rs.100
39.	SELF REALISATION	- Al Drucker	Rs. 35

OUR PUBLICATIONS ...

40.SATVIC FOOD & HEALTH (Second Revised Edition)	- Gerard T. Satvic	Rs. 40
41.SAI SANDESH	- Sai Usha	Rs. 50
42.SAI MY DIVINE BELOVED	- Sai Usha	Rs. 50
43.SATHYA SAI'S ANUGRAHA VARSHINI (Second Edition)	- Sudha Aditya	Rs. 90
44.SATHYA SAI'S AMRITA VARSHINI (Second Edition)	- Sudha Aditya	Rs. 75
45.SRI SATHYA SAI CHALEESA	- B.P. Mishra	Rs. 15
46.SATVIC STORIES	- Benjamin Kurzweil	Rs. 40
47.SAI HUMOUR	- Peggy Mason & Others	Rs. 70
48.SCRIPTURES ARE FULFILLED	- Kristina Gale-Kumar	Rs.160
49.SPRINKLES OF GOLDEN DUST	- Jeannette Caruth	Rs. 65
50.SRI SATHYA SAI BABA AND WONDERS OF HIS LOVE	- John Elliott	Rs. 90
51.SONG BIRD	- LightStorm	Rs. 60
52.SRI SATHYA SAI BABA PRAYER BOOK		Rs. 10
53.SRI SATHYA SAI BABA YOUNG ADULTS PROGRAMME	- L.A. Ramdath	Rs. 80
54.SPIRITUAL IMPRESSIONS A BI-MONTHLY MAGAZINE		Rs.100
55.STUDY CIRCLES FOR DIVINITY	- Ross Woodward & Ron Farmer	Rs.390
56.THE ARMOUR OF SRI SATHYA SAI	- O. P. Vidyakar	Rs. 10
57.THE OMNIPRESENCE OF SAI	- R. Lowenberg	Rs.120
58.THE PHOENIX RETURNS	- Kristina Gale-Kumar	Rs.250
59.THE PROPHECY	- Barbara Gardner	Rs.120
60.TEN STEPS TO KESAVA	- Johnima Wintergate	Rs.150
61.THY WILL BE DONE	- C.D. Mirchandani	Rs. 90
62.WAITING FOR BABA (Reprint)	- V. Ramnath	Rs. 95

FORTHCOMING PUBLICATIONS ...

01.A JOURNEY TO LOVE (Telugu)	- David Bailey
02.ANOTHER JOURNEY TO LOVE	- Faye Bailey
03.AT THE FEET OF SAI	- R. Lowenberg
04.DIRECTORY OF MASTERS,SAINTS, ASHRAMS AND HOLY PLACES IN INDIA	- R.Padmanaban
05.VOICE OF THE AVATAR 1994	- Sri Sathya Sai Baba
06.VOICE OF THE AVATAR 1995	- Sri Sathya Sai Baba
07.VOICE OF THE AVATAR 1996	- Sri Sathya Sai Baba
08.FACE TO FACE WITH GOD	- V.I.K. Sarin
09.FOUNTAIN OF LOVE - An Overview of Sathya Sai Water Supply Project	
10.GLORY OF SAI PADHUKAS	
11.HOLY MISSION DIVINE VISION	- Sai Usha

12.KRISHNAMURTHI AND THE FOURTH WAY - Evan Gras
13.RAJU GOES TO SCHOOL
14.SAI BABA AND GOLDEN LINGAM - Murthy
15.SAI DARSHAN - Vimla Sahni
16.SAI's STORY - Shaila Hattiangadi
17.SAI NAAMAAVALI - Jagat Narain Tripathi
18.THE ESSENTIAL REALITY OF ALL GOD FORMS - O. P. Vidyakar
19.THE HEART OF SAI - R. Lowenberg
20.THE GRACE OF SAI - R. Lowenberg
21.YOGA THERAPY - R. Lowenberg
22.SANSKRIT-ENGLISH- DICTIONARY
23.ENGLISH BHAJANS
24.INDIAN BHAJANS

Books are despatched by Registered Book Post. Copies can be had by sending Money Order/International Money Order/Demand Draft drawn in favour of SRI SATHYA SAI TOWERS HOTELS PVT. LTD Payable at any Bank at Bangalore or Prasanthi Nilayam, addressed to Sai Towers, 3/497, Main Road, Prasanthi Nilayam - 515 134, India.

POSTAGE :-

India :- At the rate of 50 ps. per 100 gms. plus Rs.12/- for Registration. Maximum 5 KG. Packing and Forwarding charges per parcel is Rs.40/-

Overseas:- 5 KGS by Sea Mail to North America, South America, Europe Rs.171 Singapore, Malaysia, Australia etc. Rs.147/- plus packing and forwarding Rs.60 per parcel.

NOTE :-

***THE PRICES SHOWN ABOVE WERE CORRECT AT THE TIME OF GOING TO PRESS, IT MAY DIFFER FROM THOSE PREVIOUSLY ADVERTISED.**